50 Ways to Love Your In-Laws

SARAH CLINE, PH.D.

Contents

Introduction

Welcome to *50 Ways to Love Your In-Laws*, a little guide truly designed to help you discover the joy, fulfillment, and satisfaction that a healthy relationship with your in-laws can offer. Of course, playing nice with the in-laws isn't always a breeze. Whether your in-laws are people you feel stuck with or you already have a decent relationship, this guide will help you navigate the trenches, learning to love and accept one another as you continue to journey through life. In these pages, you'll find insights, techniques, and inspiration to cultivate a deeper appreciation for them, including how to not only appreciate the relationship you already have with them but find ways to build upon it.

Life is a journey filled with ups and downs and twists and turns, but within every moment lies the potential for growth, connection, and joy. Whether you're seeking to enhance or strengthen your relationship with your in-laws or develop one from scratch, this book is here to act as a compass.

You will learn that through the exploration of positivity and communication within your relationships, you can uncover the keys to unlocking a life filled with a lot to be grateful for and leading to an abundance of contentment and enjoyment for years to come. Each chapter offers valuable insight and practical strategies to help grow your relationship with your in-laws and keep you and your spouse happy for years to come.

As you embark on this journey, remember that the path to loving others is unique to you. Embrace each lesson with an open mind and a willing heart. Trust that by investing in your relationship with your in-laws and prioritizing what truly matters, you'll create a life that brings you deep fulfillment and happiness.

So, without further ado, let's dive in and discover how to love your in-laws.

Love Your In-Laws By Being Positive

Imagine waking up each morning with a sense of excitement and anticipation for the day that lies ahead of you. Picture feeling energized, motivated, and ready to tackle whatever challenges come your way rather than sluggish and groggy. This is the power of positivity. The ability to approach life with optimism can truly turn even the most mundane situations into opportunities for growth and fulfillment.

In this chapter, we explore the profound psychological benefits of maintaining a positive outlook on your everyday life. From improved mental and physical well-being to enhanced relationships and greater resilience in the face of adversity, merely being positive about life and its circumstances has the potential to enrich every aspect of your time on earth. The hope is that once you read through this chapter, you will have the knowledge and expertise to cultivate a more powerful mindset so that you can breathe more positivity and embrace each day from now on with enthusiasm and gratitude. If you're interested in learning what harnessing the power of positivity has to do with your relationship with your in-laws, then join us in a complete walkthrough.

The Benefits of Positive Thinking

Of course, we all know it's better to be positive. We have heard it throughout our lifetimes. But why is it important to try and remain optimistic?

Research has shown that taking on a positive outlook can have a huge impact on mental and physical health. When you focus on the good things in your life rather than the negative, you open the door to:

- **Reduced stress and anxiety.** Lower levels of stress hormones, such as cortisol, as well as reduced symptoms of anxiety and depression, have been linked to those with a more positive outlook. This suggests that cultivating a more optimistic mindset in our daily lives offers a better coping mechanism to life's challenges, which can, in turn, aid in navigating stressful situations with greater ease.

- **Improved physical health.** Overall better health comes from positivity too! Studies have shown a link between being positive and having lower blood pressure, stronger immune function, and even a reduction in heart disease and stroke.

- **Greater resilience.** Just because you're positive doesn't mean you ignore the fact that problems do exist, or that you go through life with rose-colored glasses. It merely involves approaching life's challenges with a mindset full of resilience and optimism. When you maintain a positive outlook, you can quickly bounce back from setbacks, allowing you to overcome obstacles with more ease.

- **Stronger relationships.** Being a Debbie Downer usually is a turn-off for others. Having and maintaining a positive attitude can improve your relationships because it makes you more approachable; and besides, happy people enjoy the company of other happy people. Attitude is often contagious.

Ways to Cultivate Positivity

While some individuals may naturally possess a sunny disposition, being positive is a skill that can be cultivated and developed over time. Fortunately for all of those naturally pessimistic folks out there, there are techniques and exercises to help you foster a more positive outlook on life.

- **Practice gratitude.** First and foremost, it is important to take each day as it is and spend a few moments each day reflecting on things you are grateful for. It's easy to focus on the negative, but switch gears and take a look around. Is it a beautiful day? Are you in the company of friends, family, or significant other? Maybe you're getting that take-out dish you have been craving all week. Whatever the case, make sure you note the good. Keeping a gratitude journal can be a powerful way to do this.

- **Reframe negative thoughts.** Setbacks happen. When you're faced with them, try reframing the thoughts in a way that's more positive. Rather than dwelling on what went wrong, try and focus on something you learned instead, and how you might grow and improve in the future.

- **Surround yourself with positivity.** Try and find something that makes you feel good about your situation. Music, books, or spending time with loved ones are all great sources of inspiration. By surrounding yourself with these positive forces, you help reinforce optimism.

- **Practice self-care.** This is something often forgotten because our society has placed a selfishness stigma on regular self-care. However, taking care of your physical, emotional, and mental well-being is crucial for maintaining a positive outlook. You have to make time for activities that bring you joy and relaxation; otherwise, you'll feel burned out and oftentimes garner depression. So, no matter what it is that you can find that helps—whether it's going for a walk in nature, prayer, meditation, or indulging in hobbies—make sure that you make time for those types of enjoyment.

By practicing all of this and truly learning what it means to live positively, you can grow your relationship with anyone. Even your in-laws!

Key Takeaways

Chapter 1: The Power of Positivity underscores the potential of positivity in daily life and how it might easily be one of the biggest cornerstones of learning to love your life. By embracing optimism, individuals can enhance their mental and physical well-being, foster stronger relationships, and build resilience even in the face of adversity.

Maintaining a positive outlook has been linked to reduced stress and anxiety levels, improved physical health, greater resilience, and stronger interpersonal connections. This means that positivity has huge power, and although some people may naturally possess a positive disposition, positivity is a skill that can be developed over time. Techniques such as practicing gratitude, reframing negative thoughts, surrounding yourself with positive influences, and prioritizing self-care can all aid in fostering a more optimistic mindset. By integrating these practices into daily life, you can harness the power of positivity and navigate challenges with resilience, appreciate life's blessings, and approach each day with newfound love. This love can rub off on those around you, strengthening your relationships—even the ones you have with your in-laws!

Chapter 2

Communicate with the In-Laws

Effective communication is the foundation of any healthy relationship, whether it is a romantic relationship, a parent/child relationship, or yes, a relationship with your in-laws.

Communication is the bridge that connects us all. It enables us to come to a mutual understanding and build a stronger bond.

In this chapter, we'll delve into the essential components of communication that can strengthen the bond you have with your in-laws. Moreover, the chapter will navigate ways to validate your in-laws, yourself, and each of your needs.

While it's easy to be swayed by the idea that love is some mysterious force beyond our control, the reality is that maintaining lasting relationships requires a lot more than just love. It requires conscious effort, respect, and a willingness to understand one another on a deeper level. Depending on your in-laws and the circumstances surrounding your current relationship, this may be difficult, but by reading this guide, you've already taken a critical first step.

The truth of the matter is that the journey to love begins with appreciation, and appreciation cannot exist without communication. Appreciation also goes beyond knowing your in-laws' favorite things or doing what you think will make them happy. It's about diving deep into their psyche (and yours), comprehending their unique personality traits (and yours), and recognizing how their attributes interact with yours in a way that can formulate a healthy and lasting relationship. All of which goes right back to communication and learning about one another on a deeper level.

In the age of digital connection and instant gratification, we sometimes forget the beauty of human interaction. We often overlook the importance of patience, reflection, and presence with our loved ones. At times, we also let external factors beyond that pull us away from what truly matters. Thus, you can pause, reflect, and feel as we progress through this chapter. By fostering an environment of open communication and mutual respect, you're not just building relationships and bonds, but cultivating relationships that thrive on understanding, compassion, and genuine connection. Using this guide, you can learn how to not just communicate with your in-laws but do so effectively.

Begin Healthy Communication Rituals

Expressing your feelings is crucial for any relationship, and while that doesn't sound like a walk in the park with your in-laws, it's essential. But more than that, it is also crucial to do without triggering conflicts. It's easy to get wrapped up in emotions when expressing them to someone else, especially when you're first sorting through them, so it's critical to take a step back, breathe, and formulate thoughts before verbalizing them. Don't get caught up in name-calling or communicating to hurt someone. Remember, these are your in-laws, and no matter how you feel about them, you need to do your best to provide harmony and improve your relationship.

Sometimes tensions are high, and unfortunately, this is especially typical when families become blended, which is exactly what happened when you married your spouse, mixed their family with yours, and created a union. As an adult, you may think now is the time to lay everything out on the table and stick to your guns. While this can be true—and even beneficial for your mental wellbeing in some areas—it is important to understand how to do it in a healthy way that makes sense. To avoid as much conflict as possible, make sure to keep the heightened emotions to a minimum.

Establish Open Communication

Effective and open communication is foundational to the success of your family. Keep in mind that it can be a challenging adjustment for parents when their child marries someone, and it doesn't matter if they're liked or not liked. It's an adjustment regardless, and the relationship between your in-laws and your partner before your marriage may determine how difficult the adjustment is. Keep in mind it isn't just your in-laws going through this adjustment, either. It's also your partner. When you empathize with everyone, it can be easier to establish communication.

Start with these steps.

- **Agree to talk.** Agree to speak openly with your in-laws (and your spouse). Be clear, concise, and honest that you want to open the floor to communication. Make sure that your discussion spot is private to avoid distraction. This will help keep the conversation on its course and eliminate outward opinion or input. Remember that listening is essential to good communication.

- **Share emotions.** Make sure you're open about everything you're feeling during the conversation, including grievances, adjustments, or things you enjoy about your in-laws. It all depends on you, them, and your relationship. The most important thing is to support your in-laws (and partner) through their varied emotions and allow them to do the same. Always remember that bottling up emotions is unhealthy and counterintuitive to open communication. Encourage your in-laws to speak freely and agree to treat them with respect and patience. Reassure them that there's a safe space in your communication for them to be honest and open.

- **Value and respect every member of the conversation.** This includes your in-laws, your partner, and yourself. Keep both your mind and the communication floor open to all members of the conversation. This will help everyone stay connected.

Your compassion is essential in helping your family and your in-laws feel welcome and wanted. Some additional ways to effectively open the door to open communication are by setting clear boundaries, which we will discuss later.

Setting limits with children helps them to feel a sense of security, and the same can be said for adults, specifically your in-laws (or even your own parents). When someone understands where a boundary line lies, they feel secure knowing that when they operate within those limits, everyone remains happy and satisfied.

Remain Calm

Try not to overreact to difficult situations. By remaining calm, it's more likely that your in-laws will respect you enough to see it from your perspective.

Express Feelings With Words, Not Actions

If you start to get angry and feel you may lose control, take a break and do something to help yourself feel calm.

- Take a walk

- Do breathing exercises

- Interact with a pet

- Journal

- Read a book

Address One Issue at a Time

Only introduce lesser issues once the primary problem has been fully discussed. This way, you'll avoid what experts call the kitchen sink effect. Dr. John Mordechai Gottman (born April 26, 1942), an American psychologist and professor at the University of Washington, coined the term to describe the act of one person throwing "everything but the kitchen sink" into a discussion or argument by dredging up past mistakes and grievances. This tactic is particularly counterproductive because it's often overwhelming to the person receiving the grievances. This is especially true of your in-laws. Even if you have grievances about your spouse's childhood or if there are recent (or even current) issues, avoid bringing them all up during a time of argument or debate. These are better suited to be included in planned discussions. Family therapy sessions are especially helpful in these sorts of situations.

Resist Underhandedness

Avoid hitting below the belt or being underhanded. Tensions can be high in this sort of a relationship, and it may seem easy to hit below the belt when upset, but don't use conversations—or any situation—as an excuse to attack your in-laws, no matter how easy it may seem or how much you want to cause them emotional harm in the moment. The goal is to build a stronger relationship, not damage the one you have. Remember, you could easily trigger sensitive areas or potentially hurt their feelings, and although this may be tempting at the moment, don't give in to the temptation. These attacks only foster distrust, anger, and harmful vulnerability. The goal isn't to "win" arguments. We want to work through issues by effectively communicating. Being underhanded is not effective communication.

Avoid Clamming Up

When having a conversation with someone, especially your in-laws, tensions can rise. It's easy to feel emotionally charged when discussing your feelings, especially with your in-laws. When emotions run high, we, as humans, tend to "clam up" or shut down.

It's important to note that when one person becomes silent and stops responding, frustration and anger can quickly follow. If you feel overwhelmed or as though you're shutting down, you may need to take a break from the discussion. Simply ask to take a break and excuse yourself. Just remember to follow up on the discussion later. Likewise, respect the fact that it may be your in-laws who need the space. If they ask for a break, give it to them.

Be Specific and Productive

Be precise if there is something that is bothering you. Try not to generalize. Avoid words like *never* or *always*. These sweeping terms are usually inaccurate anyway and will (almost) always heighten tensions. Instead of using hyperbolic language, focus on what you're feeling in the moment due to a specific event. Vague complaints are challenging to address, so tackling each specific item productively is important.

Share Your Feelings

Human beings are social creatures. Because of this, there is no good that can come from struggling alone. Sharing your feelings with others is vital to a healthy mental wellbeing. Your in-laws can be great supporters, and the relationships you have with them can benefit from sharing your feelings. Whether it's your feelings on them specifically or more in-depth feelings in general, consider sharing.

If there is something specific that you've learned about them during your open-communication ventures, or even something you have learned about yourself, be honest about how you feel about it or if there is an issue you're struggling with.

Use Neutral Language to Curb Defensiveness

Your choice of words can significantly impact the tone of your communication. To prevent defensiveness and promote understanding, avoid accusatory language and instead focus on the specific behavior or issue. Accusations will lead your in-laws to focus on defending themselves rather than understanding you or your perspective. Instead, discuss how an action made you feel.

Use "We" Statements

Using "we" instead of "you" statements conveys that you are in this together, working as a team to resolve a problem. It's important to communicate that you are practicing empathy and acknowledging their feelings and perspectives.

Don't Say This

"You never listen to anyone else. It's always about what you want."

Instead, Say This

"We seem to have a disconnect sometimes in our communication."

Emphasizing "we" makes the conversation more about finding solutions together rather than pointing fingers. It can often lead to a more productive and less confrontational discussion.

Use "I" Statements

Expressing yourself without becoming overly aggressive can be challenging when faced with a conflict, especially if your in-laws are pushing your buttons or have been acting out a lot recently. To help de-escalate the situation and clarify your point, an "I" or assertive statement is an effective psychiatrist-approved approach. Suppose there's a conflict where you feel your in-laws are always getting involved with your life in ways you don't necessarily want them to be involved.

Don't Say This

"You are always butting in."

Instead, Say This

"I feel a little overwhelmed when you assert your opinion or offer unsolicited advice. I would like us to set boundaries for this so we can always be on the same page."

This "I" statement expresses your feelings and needs without blaming or accusing them. After all, if you're having this conversation, it's because your in-laws are wanting to help—even when you don't want them to. Using language that emphasizes how you feel is much more effective communication and is less likely to result in them shutting down or getting angry. It also aids in their ability to empathize and see things from your perspective. Here's another example.

Don't Say This
"You never listen." (This is also likely a generalization.)

Instead, Say This
"I feel frustrated when I feel unheard. I would like it if we worked on listening to each other a little more effectively."

Speaking this way avoids tactics of attack, critique, and criticism, which usually lead to more hostility and defensiveness. In general, using "I" messages can create a constructive dialogue about the true causes of any conflict by avoiding aggressive behaviors and fostering effective communication.

Listen Actively

Practice active listening when your in-laws communicate with you. Avoid interrupting them when they're speaking, even if you disagree. This may be difficult, but active listening is the cornerstone of all effective communication—and relationships in general. It involves not only hearing the words they say but also understanding their emotions and perspectives. Validate them and show them that you're listening by maintaining eye contact and providing non-verbal cues like nodding. Our body language matters.

Be present in the conversation, and take their feelings and criticisms seriously. Don't be distracted by external forces. Never multitask while someone is communicating with you. Listen to and reflect on what they are saying before responding. Be sure to ask open-ended questions to encourage them to share more, and remember this rule: if they are communicating it, it's important.

Share Memories

Sharing memories is a great communication tool and also a wonderful way to bond. Sharing memories can be uplifting and create a calming effect. Studies show that sharing memories can boost a person's mood and counteract negative emotions and even illness. Reminiscing has been proven to increase feelings of joy, which in turn causes your brain to function better. When your mood perks up, your brain does, too. In fact, your brain and body enter a state of positive affect and positive activation. Here are examples of great memories to share.

- A beloved memory of your kids

- A favorite pet, especially if your in-laws knew them

- Summer vacations or other fun trips you might have taken together

- Your wedding to their child (your spouse)

Other ways to share memories are by:

- Making family-favorite meals

- Watching old movies everyone enjoys

- Listening to special songs

Ultimately, there is no hard and fast rule on how to share memories with one another. The important thing is to just do it.

Ask About Their Day

Everyone's life is busy. Between balancing your job, family needs, house needs, and your own needs, it can often be difficult to remember to make time for other extended family members, especially in-laws.

But this is where you have to worry about taking someone you care about for granted. Oftentimes, the change from someone holding a key spot in your life to becoming somewhat of a secondary role happens gradually—so gradually that it's difficult to see it happening. Whether your in-laws have been a key speaker in your life or not doesn't matter. The fact of the matter is, they used to hold a key spot in your partner's life.

They're your partner's parents.

Even if your in-laws drive you insane, it's important to remember that.

A great way to prevent moving them into a secondary role is to set a little time aside every so often to communicate and emotionally connect. According to research, friendship is essential to all satisfying and healthy relationships. We always greet our friends with questions on their days–the same can be true for our in-laws.

Express Affection

This may or may not be part of your everyday behavior with your in-laws. Either you are affectionate or you aren't, but it is important that no matter what, you do show them some affection. This guide will aid in ways to do that appropriately. So don't worry! If you're not the type to be affectionate with your in-laws, there will be techniques to use without making it weird.

So why should you be affectionate with your in-laws? There are many benefits of expressing and receiving affection, no matter what the relationship dynamic is.

Here are some of the most common.

- **It increases oxytocin levels.** Oxytocin is a hormone and neurotransmitter that plays a crucial role in various physiological and social functions in humans and other animals. It is often referred to as the "love hormone" or even the "bonding hormone" because of its role in facilitating social bonding, trust, and attachment between individuals. Overall, oxytocin is a crucial component of human social behavior and plays a significant role in shaping our relationships and emotional experiences.

- **It reduces stress.** Studies show that affection lowers cortisol levels, which is the key hormone related to our bodies' stress response. This means that affection lowers stress.

- **Affection is great for mental health.** People in affectionate relationships of all shapes and sizes experience fewer mental health issues, such as anxiety and depression, as compared to those who are in overall unhealthy relationships.

- **It can improve physical health.** If something as small as a simple hug can boost your immune responses and reduce illness severity, wouldn't you be interested to see how much maintaining actively affectionate relationships can improve your long-term wellness and the wellness of your family/friends?

It's possible to get too much of a good thing, though. Make sure you avoid going too far and forcing affection. The goal is to strengthen your relationship, not be invasive or unwelcome. Balance is everything.

Share Personal Growth Moments

Using feedback obtained from your open communication times, you can begin to document your personal development. It's important to truly listen to what others have to say about you and implement changes appropriately. For example, if someone tells you that you get angry quickly, learning a few meditation techniques may be helpful. If you've successfully navigated an emotionally heightened situation since then and didn't blow your top, this might be a great personal growth moment to share with your loved ones, including your in-laws.

Of course, everyone's relationships are different. It's entirely possible that you don't want the kind of dynamic with your in-laws in which you feel the need to disclose *all* of your personal growth, especially if you feel it somehow makes you overly vulnerable. That's fine. Just make sure you're sharing some growth moments. Your in-laws want to know that you're continually growing in life. Otherwise, wouldn't they fear that their child is somehow stuck in a web of complacency with you?

Talk to the in-laws about whatever level of growth you want. This could be a personal record at the gym, a new skill learned at work, etc. And if you use techniques such as journaling, you'll have a great record of feedback and your own reflections. These can truly provide a glimpse of previous versions of yourself and give greater insight into your personal growth.

Personal growth is an ongoing journey. Share these moments of realization—even epiphanies—with your loved ones. Discuss your personal experiences, challenges, and lessons learned through self-reflection and check-ins with your in-laws (more about emotional check-ins later). Nothing feels better than knowing we've helped someone, so when your in-laws help you out, be sure to tell them!

Along the way, support one another's aspirations and encourage continued self-improvement exercises. Then go on to celebrate milestones in your personal development journey together. By following these guidelines and strategies, you can improve your communication with your in-laws, no matter what your relationship already looks like. Effective communication is the key to understanding, empathy, and building a strong and thriving relationship.

Forgive and Make Peace with the Past

Forgiveness isn't easy. However, it is often a crucial task—or, at least, it should be. When we become adults, it's easy to blame our parents—and our in-laws for that matter—for things that happened during our or our spouse's childhoods. Perhaps your partner has told you they didn't always have a good relationship with their parents, or maybe they harbor so much negative emotion over something that happened that they have prevented the relationship from fully blossoming. It's even possible that your in-laws have done something negative since they became their in-laws, whether that be to you, your partner, or your kids.

Whatever the case, learning to forgive people is a necessary part of your mental health, and forgiving your in-laws is no exception. There are three key steps to forgiving.

1. Let go of past resentments.

2. Develop realistic expectations.

3. Cherish the good.

Let Go of Past Resentments

Having on-going resentments toward someone else does more than just keep them in the doghouse. In fact, it keeps *you* from truly feeling free, too. As human beings, we forever have a victim mentality, and clinging to issues from our past is a way of keeping them with us forever.

No matter how upset you are with your in-laws, it's important to recognize that you need to resolve those resentments and move forward. This is true whether you want a relationship going forward or not.

Develop Realistic Expectations

If there are unresolved issues from your past that you need to forgive, make sure you're setting realistic expectations not only for your in-laws, but for yourself, your partner, everyone's healing, and the relationship itself. If there were/are a lot of toxicity issues, it's entirely possible that having a close and healthily functioning relationship is not practical without a lot of family counseling. Consider this when setting your expectations. On the flip side, though, if you don't have a lot of personal resentments, make sure you're not setting the bar too low, especially if you want a relationship with your in-laws.

Communicate Boundaries

As dynamics shift (for example, when you got married to your partner, your dynamic shifted, and so did the role each of you had with both sets of parents), so should your boundaries. But what are normal boundaries to have as an adult with your parents and in-laws?

These include having your own space and being seen as an adult capable of making decisions on your own. It also includes your parents and in-laws recognizing that the primary family dynamic is now you, your partner, and your children (if you have them). This can be a difficult adjustment, but it is completely necessary.

Healthy boundaries include discussing these shifts in dynamics as well as appreciating one another completely. Appreciating one another means valuing and respecting each other's time and feeling safe enough to share sensitive information. Your in-laws and your own parents must understand that you and your partner are not children anymore and can enforce limits as you see fit.

Here are a few common boundaries you should set with your in-laws.

- Request that they call before they come over.

- Tell them that you don't want unsolicited relationship or marriage advice.

- Avoid commenting on your life choices just because they disagree with them.

- Ask that they understand that you and your partner have additional priorities.

- Request physical space to be a family unit without them from time to time.

- Ask that they not invade your privacy.

Is It Disrespectful to Set Boundaries with Parents and In-Laws?

Some people may worry that setting boundaries with their parents and in-laws is considered disrespectful. Boundaries set by adult children *can* feel disrespectful to some parents and in-laws, making you feel worse for enforcing them. But it's still important to set them because although it may seem disrespectful, it isn't. It's healthy and it's natural.

General Tips to Set Boundaries with Parents and In-Laws

If you are unsure where to start when setting boundaries with your parents, start with these basics.

- **Know your limits.** Knowing your limits is the first step in setting boundaries. If you know what boundaries you need and know your in-laws may violate them, it's better to be proactive than reactive. It's also best to discuss the potential consequences of violating these boundaries.

- **Let go of guilt over having boundaries.** Guilting yourself for wanting or having boundaries is putting yourself through tough emotions twice. There is no need for that! Your needs are valid.

- **Be direct.** Although this may be challenging, especially in young adulthood, being direct about your feelings truly can go a long way. If you tiptoe around the issue, you're not helping anyone because you likely aren't being honest. Your in-laws ultimately cannot read your mind. They will never know what is necessary if you aren't honest and open.

- **Know when you need space.** Knowing when you need a time-out is vital. If you need space or alone time, that is nothing to feel guilty about. Communicate those needs with your parents to ensure everyone is at full mental capacity and health when you come together.

Set Boundaries for Your In-Laws During Major Transitions

It's critical to speak to your in-laws about specific ground rules. If you are going to live with them, though (or they live with you), it's even more important to discuss the living arrangements, rules, and responsibilities beforehand to help prevent misunderstandings. We all want comfortable living situations, and open communication is key here.

Consider questions such as:

- How much should I/you contribute?

- How long will we be in the same household? Estimate this as closely as possible.

- How much privacy is needed for each person?

Clear communication not only helps you share your intentions but also prevents unwanted surprises and potentially strained relationships as a result. Establishing boundaries within the home, such as the need for personal space and when it is appropriate to interact with one another, can help maintain a peaceful space. By communicating effectively and respecting each other's boundaries, you can build trust and strengthen your relationship with your parents.

In a regular roommate situation, it's normal to come to some sort of agreement on rules for the house as well as the people residing within. It's normal to discuss responsibilities and expectations, especially before moving in together. So do the same with your in-laws, whether you're living with them or they're living with you. Set aside time to have a serious conversation on past issues that might need to be dealt with, obstacles you anticipate in the future, and how your day-to-day living situation will look.

For example, work out how much each party will pay in rent, bills, and other costs. Work out that plan ahead of time and try to get a game plan on how long you intend to live together.

If you're not living with your in-laws at all, it's still crucial that you set some sort of boundaries, especially as you transition into creating your own family.

Respect Their Space and Yours

No matter where you are in your life, it's important that you're giving others and yourself much-needed space. This not only helps you recoup and avoid burnout from your relationships, but it also gives you time to reflect on yourself. If your in-laws come to visit, welcome them warmly, but if the visits become too frequent, make sure you're communicating appropriate boundaries and timeframe expectations for visiting and/or going out together. If you live with them or they live with you, show respect for their space. When you're in their rooms, try to make them feel like you are visiting their house. Likewise, ask them to respect your space as well. Communicate where boundaries need to be and what works best for your family. Make sure you all respect your individual needs and give each other space when necessary.

Have Emotional Check-Ins

We have discussed emotional check-ins previously in this guide, and it's important to define what an emotional check-in is and what it does.

Check-ins can be just to see how your loved ones are doing, or they can hold deeper meaning. Ultimately, though, they are great times to do reflection exercises and truly delve into one another's wellbeing and psyche. If you have set boundaries with your in-laws recently or vice versa, discuss together how everything is going in these meetings.

Schedule Personal Time for Reflection and Understanding

Allocating time for personal reflection and understanding enhances self-awareness and empathy. It gives time for each person to discover their unique needs as well as their strengths and weaknesses. Admitting personal faults to ourselves, let alone others, isn't easy. So consider setting aside moments for self-reflection. Specialists also recommend you journal these thoughts to better understand your emotions and to have the ability to look back at your progress. Encourage your family members to do the same. Share your insights with one another when you're ready.

Use this personal time to explore your progress and how those advancements align with your in-laws' journeys of self-awareness. Self-awareness refers to a clear understanding of your own emotions, strengths, weaknesses, thoughts, and beliefs and how they might influence your behavior, including your interactions with others. Being self-aware is fundamental for healthy relationships with yourself and others. Understanding ourselves means understanding our needs, expectations, boundaries, and communication styles. All of these shape how we interact and love our family members and friends. When we're not self-aware, we open the door to harmful interactions due to blind spots in our communication and waning emotional health. A lack of self-awareness can lead to many unfortunate states.

- **Poor emotional regulation,** which results in outbursts and other unhealthy expressions of anger or hurt.

- **Personal neglect and impaired mental health**

- **A skewed perception of reality** due to biases and defense mechanisms that build up over time. (Also, without self-awareness, a person tends to reject constructive criticism, thus missing out on potential personal growth.)

- **Communication blind spots**

- **Crossing boundaries,** whether your own or others' boundaries.

Being more self-aware gives us the tools necessary to have satisfying and successful relationships. It just makes sense. Know yourself, and you'll have the foundation for a life and relationship that isn't just surviving but thriving.

Avoid Toxicity

It's important to know when a relationship is toxic. Toxic relationships should be avoided at all costs, and one of the best indicators of toxicity is if the other person is willing to admit fault and work on your relationship or if they gaslight you into thinking everything is always your fault.

Navigating healthy relationships involves recognizing and steering clear of toxic dynamics. Toxicity in relationships can manifest in various forms, including emotional manipulation, lack of respect, dishonesty, and constant negativity. The importance of avoiding toxicity cannot be overstated, as it can severely impact mental and emotional well-being and then lead to stress, anxiety, depression, and even physical health issues.

One crucial aspect of avoiding toxicity is establishing and maintaining boundaries. Healthy boundaries are essential for defining acceptable behavior and protecting your own (and your family's) emotional and mental space. Without clear boundaries, you may find yourself tolerating mistreatment.

Communication also plays a pivotal role in mitigating any sort of toxicity in relationships. Open and honest communication can truly allow you to express your needs, concerns, and boundaries effectively. Additionally, being self-aware is also key to recognizing and addressing toxic patterns within yourself.

If you feel you're contributing to the toxicity in a relationship, it's time to take a step back and reflect on how to work toward your own personal growth and develop healthier ways to interact with others.

Key Takeaways

Effective communication forms the foundation of all healthy and flourishing relationships. This chapter has explored how you might engage with your in-laws on a deeper level and communicate about issues that you may have with them or the past you share.

Start difficult discussions by expressing feelings without instigating conflicts. No matter what happens, it is important to remain calm and collect yourself before delving headfirst into the conversation. Remember, others are a lot more likely to consider your perspective if they feel that they can voice their concerns without you jumping off the deep end or responding out of anger and vice versa.

Here are several of the best ways to express yourself without conflict.

- **Express feelings with words, not actions.** If you feel anger rising to an uncontrollable level, take a step back and return to the conversation after you've calmed down. Consider engaging in other activities that help you regain your composure. Encourage your in-laws to do the same. Use methods like walking, deep breathing, or journaling to manage strong emotions constructively.

- **Address one issue at a time.** Avoid resorting to the kitchen sink approach. Focus on one issue at a time when discussing conflicts.

- **Resist underhandedness.** Steer clear of using underhanded or hurtful tactics when discussing sensitive topics with your in-laws. Attacking them in sensitive areas only fosters distrust, anger, and vulnerability, which is counterproductive to communication.

- **Be specific and productive.** When expressing concerns, be specific and avoid making generalized statements using words like *never* or *always*. Broad complaints are challenging to address and usually aren't even true.

Once all of you can communicate effectively, make sure that you demonstrate active listening skills during conversations and use neutral language. "I" and "we" statements are best employed to emphasize that you are working together for a common goal and not attacking them.

It's important to note that some people may be a little less vocal during communication, and that's okay! Appreciate the silence. Allow them the space and time to collect their thoughts and feelings. Avoid pressuring them to speak immediately after a conflict, and create a safe environment where silence is just considered a part of the communication process.

Other people, on the other hand, don't do as well with silence. Make sure that you are offering verbal affirmations to help them feel safe and loved during communication. Compliment them genuinely.

The next thing we learned about is how the dynamic may shift as you, your in-laws, and your partner grow older. Recognizing that the relationships you have with your in-laws (and the one your partner has with their parents) evolve. Remember that this transition can take a bit of adjustment but can eventually lead to an even stronger bond than before (for you, your partner, and the in-laws). This is especially true if boundaries are respected as certain transitions occur.

Remember to deal with any past or unresolved issues respectfully and check in with your in-laws often after important conversations or boundaries are set just to get an idea of how everyone is feeling and gauge how everyone feels it's going.

Make sure you schedule personal time for reflection and communicate your findings with your family, too, during regular emotional check-ins; and finally, respect one another and the space that you all may need individually.

By following these guidelines and strategies, you can improve your communication with your stepparent, fostering understanding, empathy, and a strong, thriving relationship as you navigate the shifting dynamics of your relationship.

Learn to Appreciate Them

In Chapter 3 of our guide, we delve into the importance of appreciating our in-laws for who they are and what they have to offer. Currently. Not in the future.

While it's true that you're reading this guide to grow a stronger bond with your in-laws, it's important to learn to appreciate them for who they are today as well as the relationship you have with them today. This chapter explores various aspects of building and maintaining a strong emotional connection with your in-laws and highlights the value of learning to appreciate them regardless.

Express Your Appreciation

Expressing appreciation toward your in-laws is essential to nurturing positive relationships and fostering a sense of mutual respect and gratitude within your extended family. It's important to reflect on moments worthy of conveying gratitude for and then share that gratitude with your in-laws. Expressing your appreciation for things they've done for you, whether that be through words of thanks or thoughtful gestures truly underscores the profound impact of how grateful you are.

Gratitude is a multifaceted concept with numerous definitions, but its benefits are undeniable. Research indicates that expressing gratitude not only promotes psychological, social, and physical well-being but also strengthens interpersonal bonds and enhances overall life satisfaction. The power of positivity (as discussed in Chapter 1) goes along with this. By being positive and showing gratification, we allow ourselves to live fuller and more fulfilling lives. It's a domino effect.

So how can we best express gratitude toward our in-laws?

We already know that by incorporating gratitude into our daily lives we can cultivate a habit of appreciation that enriches our relationships and contributes to our overall happiness and well-being. Actions that demonstrate gratitude hold significance. Therefore, it's essential to recognize and practice effective methods of expressing gratitude that are tailored to the social context and individual preferences of our in-laws.

To do this, it's important to:

- Offer random acts of kindness.

- Maintain respect in all interactions with them.

- Write them a letter or verbally express gratitude.

Expressing gratitude not only benefits our well-being but also strengthens social bonds and promotes prosocial behavior. Research suggests that grateful individuals are better able to form social connections, cope with stress, and maintain positive relationships. We can all use a little more of that when dealing with in-laws.

Ultimately, how you show your gratitude is up to you, but expressing it toward your in-laws is a powerful way to strengthen your familial relationships, enhance well-being, and foster a sense of connection and belonging within your extended family. By incorporating gratitude into your daily lives and finding meaningful ways to express appreciation, you can create a more positive and fulfilling family dynamic for yourself and your loved ones, including your significant other.

Nurture the Relationship You Have

Relationships aren't static. They are almost like living organisms in the way that they require a ton of attention and care in order to thrive. To benefit from strong connections with others, you should take charge of your relationships and put in the time and energy you would any other aspect of your wellbeing.

Connect With Your In-Laws

Even in the digital age, one of the biggest challenges for families is to stay connected amidst the busy pace of life. It's a shame, really, especially considering that the healthiest, longest-living people in the world all have something in common: they put family first. Research links family bonds to longevity due to the support family can provide. Families can provide comfort and support and even influence better health outcomes while sick. Experts recommend connecting with family by letting the little grievances go (i.e., picking your battles), spending time together, and expressing love and compassion to one another.

Learn to Forgive

Conflicts and breaches of trust are regular occurrences in relationships, but how you navigate the hurt that comes from them can profoundly influence the path to healing. Embracing forgiveness offers a spectrum of both physical and emotional advantages. According to researchers, releasing resentment or anguish tied to a situation becomes more attainable when you recognize that a lot of the distress stems from your own thoughts and emotions rather than just the event itself.

Be Compassionate

Compassion means to be receptive to both yourself and others even in the middle of difficulty, responding with a tender, nonjudgmental mindset. By extending compassion to another individual—be it a romantic partner, friend, family member, or coworker—you foster improved communication so you can forge deeper connections. When it comes to your in-laws, nurturing the relationship you have with them may require a bit of compassion. It doesn't mean shouldering their issues or internalizing their emotions. Instead, it involves acknowledging when they are distressed or unfulfilled and feeling compelled to offer some sort of assistance or support.

Accept Them

It is also important to be accepting of your in-laws. Obviously, this does not apply in situations of abuse or unhealthy control; in those situations, your foremost need is to protect yourself. But otherwise, try to understand where they are coming from rather than judge them or attempt to shun them when they get under your skin. Make sure that you treat them the way you want to be treated. Be patient and know that people change. Nurture the relationship, accept them as they are, and continue to communicate with them openly to strengthen the relationship and address issues.

Create and Maintain Traditions Together

With busy schedules and the presence of online social media, it's easy to let go of some of our familial responsibilities. In fact, we as a generation have opted for internet connection with our family and friends more than physical connection, which is a shame as it only offers the façade of real contact. Because of this digital age, it is quite easy to drift from family and friends. In order to nurture relationships fully, you must nurture the closeness and support of the relationship itself. In other words, you have to make an effort to connect.

In fact, research shows that people who deliberately make time for one another—for instance, through gatherings, trips, or traditions—enjoy stronger relationships and a more positive energy. An easy way to begin is to start slow. For example, if you have a ritual of going out for a walk every morning, incorporate some family time into that. Invite your in-laws to enjoy a morning stroll, and eventually, that can become a tradition that everyone genuinely cherishes.

Balance Social and Alone Time

When nurturing your relationships, it's all about balance. It's important to spend some time socializing (hanging out with family, sharing meals together, talking on the phone, etc.) but it's also equally important to spend some time alone. Research shows that people who spend six to seven hours per day socializing tend to be happier than those who don't. Likewise, those who have zero social interactions had the same result as those with an overload of social time; they were found to feel significantly more stressed than their more balanced counterparts. In essence, knowing when to give your time to others and when to save a little for yourself is crucial to your health, the health of your relationships, and your overall emotional wellbeing.

Keep Commitments

It's incredibly easy to cancel plans in today's digital world. You can even cancel a doctor's appointment through their app or portal. When you're feeling a little antisocial, with a quick text you can send a dozen excuses to a loved one about why you can't make it to whatever plan you committed to. You can just as quickly call them up and tell them a little white lie to get out of that family get-together.

However, in today's world—an age where the excuses are endless and communication is so much quicker and easier—it's that much more important to keep commitments. Keeping commitments is one of the best ways to nurture your relationships, especially the ones with your in-laws. They want to see that their child has married someone who keeps their word, and keeping commitments with them is a good indicator of how good your word truly is.

Trust is essential in all relationships, and it's important to recognize how keeping your commitments equates to being trustworthy. As children, we all learn the value of promises. In fact, a lot of our earliest disappointments reside around an adult not keeping their word, and our biggest happiness stemmed from fulfilling their word. These experiences were necessary building blocks to our foundation and taught us the power of commitment.

Remember, if you aren't one hundred percent certain that you can keep a commitment, simply don't make it. The person you're making the commitment with would likely appreciate a "maybe" or even a "no" over a broken commitment or a canceled plan.

It's perfectly natural to want to please someone else and tell them "yes" before even thinking it through. In fact, as human beings, we are constantly worried about causing frustration or disappointment to our loved ones. But understand that disappointment on the front end is much better than on the back end. This is because breaking commitments breaks trust and therefore hurts relationships in the long run.

Treat Them

Being treated is something universally pleasant. Everyone enjoys feeling special. No matter what your in-laws might fall into with their love language or personality, you can bet they would enjoy being treated from time to time.

Surprise Them With Gifts

One way to treat your in-laws is to surprise them with gifts. No need to wait on special occasions. Sometimes the best gifts are "just because" gifts. Pampering your loved ones is a great way to help them feel loved and appreciated. So, schedule a gift delivery to their home or take it to them yourself, and make them smile from ear to ear. Bringing your in-laws gifts—especially ones you put a lot of thought into, may really be a great way to show your love or appreciation for them.

In fact, some personality types crave gifts.

But sometimes, we find that in-laws are not always easy to buy for. They may already have everything they could ever want—or maybe you just really have no idea what they could really use/

enjoy. This can be for multiple reasons, but no matter the case, if you're stuck on what to buy your in-laws, think about something thoughtful and personalized!

Some ideas:

- **A personalized pillow**: Think about getting a pillow for your in-laws to put on their bed. It can have a quote or a photo of them together!

- **A personalized mug**: Do either or both of your in-laws drink coffee? Coffee mugs are some of the best gifts because everyone has them, and everyone can usually use a fun, personalized one or two! Customizing them with a photograph, a quote, or a hand-written note can go a long away—especially if they live further away than you or your spouse may like!

- **Kitchen supplies:** Think of an apron or a cutting board! Customize these with your family name or the name of all of your in-laws' children and/or grandchildren! This could be a fun, clever, and intimate gift that they could keep (and use) for the rest of their lives!

- **A doormat:** Personalized doormats are great because it's the first thing someone sees when they visit a home! Consider putting their family name as well as each individual family member's name on this, that way they feel their entire family is represented at the matriarch and patriarch home (even if they no longer share a last name with their child(ren).

- **A cookie jar:** Everyone needs a cookie jar for when kids and grandkids come over! Think of some of your in-laws' favorite things and personalize a cookie jar to match it–just make sure it doesn't clash with their kitchen aesthetics!

- **A wooden clock or a family calendar:** Consider a customized clock with family members on it, or a calendar or even a family tree with everyone listed as well as their birthdays. These kinds of gifts are three-fold. They're informational (sometimes your in-laws may need a little help remembering birthdays especially if you have a big family), they hold a practical use, and it's sweet and personalized so there's a sentimental aspect to it, too.

- **Art:** This can be something you found, something you made, or something you had made. Bring them some art to display and they'll think of you each and every time they pass it

Make a Surprise Visit to Them

If your in-laws always seem to want to spend time with you and your family and you just haven't had a lot of time, consider making a surprise visit to them and spending the weekend. They would love it, and you could get a lot of much-needed bonding time. Spend the whole weekend with them if you can, talk to them, lend a hand, and help them whenever the opportunity calls for it!

Pamper Them With Spa Day

Just because they may not be used to it or maybe have never even had it, don't sleep on the fact that a spa day is great for rejuvenating the soul! Sometimes our loved ones forget to take care of themselves. So book a spa appointment for them so you can help them to relax and recharge their batteries. Consider booking a couples spa for them, too, if they're still together, so they can spend some cozy time with one another.

Write Them Letters

Although talking to your in-laws about what you are thinking or feeling can sometimes be a challenge, it is possible to try to communicate something that is emotional by letter instead. This is also a great way to show your appreciation. Not only are you taking time out of your day to write them a letter, but you're also willing to dive into your emotional well-being and be vulnerable with them.

This can take pressure off by allowing you the outlet you need to get things off your chest, and an opportunity for them to receive the information in a private space where they can properly process their feelings. Remember, although you can do this to express your feelings on big-subject matters you don't want to discuss in person, you can also use this as a way to grow closer emotionally and the "just because".

Regardless of the subject matter, here are a few tips on how to get started.

- Organize your thoughts first! It's important to know what you want to convey to them.

- Remember that you can't take back what you write.

- Remember that this is an opportunity to share your story or feelings without distraction or interruption. Be authentic and genuine!

Cook a Meal for Them

There is an old saying, "The family that eats together, stays together." Cook for your family—whether breakfast, lunch, or dinner—and include your in-laws! Enjoy food and time together. They will certainly enjoy the time with their child and grandchildren (if you have children). This is a great opportunity to bond and spend quality time with each other and forge a truly healthy dynamic.

Experience New Hobbies Together

It is likely, especially if you're reading this, that you had a life before you met your partner and their parents (your in-laws). You probably have an abundance of memories of your own parents and others in your family. However, while revisiting memories or places that are important to your family and your past is often an emotional experience, it is still important to make sure you're making new memories together, whether you have a lot with your in-laws or don't have many at all!

Creating new memories with your in-laws is a wonderful way to strengthen your relationship. These moments can be cherished for a lifetime and can help you connect on a deeper level.

- **Travel together.** Exploring new destinations can be a fantastic way to bond with your stepparent. Whether it's a weekend getaway to a nearby town or an international adventure, traveling together allows you to share unique experiences and create lasting memories. Discovering new cultures, trying different cuisines, and exploring historic sites might be exactly what you all need to feel connected with each other and to get a jumpstart on new memories you can cherish forever.

- **Outdoor adventures.** Spend time in nature by going on hikes, camping trips, or nature walks. The great outdoors offers plenty of opportunities for bonding, and it's a chance to unplug from technology and enjoy each other's company. Consider kayaking or other on-the-lake adventures to kick it up a notch. If someone hasn't tried it, this experience can be even more enriching and mean even more!

- **Cooking and baking.** Preparing meals together can be a fun and delicious way to create memories. Consider trying to cook up a new recipe or bake homemade goodies; you can even consider making it a game. A cook-off with judges is a great way to get the entire family involved. It's a win-win. You get quality time and yummy food! And if you're competitive, it may be a chance to really show off.

- **Attend cultural events.** Explore your city or a nearby city and discover what sort of cultural scenes they have. Many cities have showcases of other cultures at various times throughout the year. Learn about some of these by searching online. You may find concerts, theater performances, art exhibits, or even full-blown cultural festivals that may be a ton of fun. Not only will these events provide opportunities to appreciate art and culture, but they can also be a great way to make a memory with your family.

- **Document the moments.** Sometimes we don't remember everything as it was. Consider taking lots of photos and videos to enhance your memories and give you a tangible piece of the memory so you can cherish that as well.

- **Volunteer together.** Giving back to the community by volunteering together is not only a meaningful way to bond but also a chance to make a positive impact on your community. Sharing this experience with your in-laws can be rewarding and create lasting memories centered around compassion and selflessness.

Find Common Ground

Journeying through life is all about exploration. If you and your in-laws came into each other's lives a long time ago, it's possible that you didn't have a lot in common initially. This could be because you were too young or the timing was simply off to truly take an interest in what they enjoyed. Whatever the case, it may be worth revisiting for the sake of finding common ground. There may be more common ground than you may think, even if you already feel you have some things in common.

The point is, whether you had anything in common or not before doesn't mean that all hope is lost in finding common interests. It could exist already or it may exist later. The truth is, there is a world of possibilities to explore now that you're older, wiser, and taking steps to grow your relationship with your in-laws. Discovering and trying new things together is a chance to bond over or develop shared interests and passions, whether you know you have them or not. The key to keeping a strong connection with them is to shuck away any notion of complacency and strive to continually grow *with* them. What better way to bring forth some freshness than to find a fun new hobby you can participate in with them?

When exploring new activities to try, consider their interests and preferences. You can take turns choosing activities with them (whether it be the two of them together or you with just one of them at a time), ensuring that you all have a say. Be open to trying things you may not have considered before; you might come to find that you enjoy something you never thought you could.

Whether it's trying a new cuisine, taking up a dance class, embarking on a road trip, or learning a new skill, the key is to approach these experiences with an open heart and mind and be willing to embrace the unknown. Know that at the end of the day, even if you don't enjoy the activity you're doing something different with your in-laws that is sure to create memories and strengthen your relationship by just spending quality time together.

Keep in mind that depending on their personality, everyone may enjoy different activities, but it's important for you all to broaden your horizons. Even if it's something you think you may not enjoy, try it! You may surprise yourself. Consider making this part of your regular scheduled time with them, and consider being the first to suggest it! Start with something you know they will enjoy getting the ball rolling.

Here are a few ideas for experiencing a new activity with your more introverted family members.

- Start a book club with them.

- Stretch it out with some yoga, whether at a studio or at home.

- Play games or do a puzzle together.

- Garden together.

- Start a collection.

- Brew beer at home.

- Learn how to knit together.

- For outgoing members of the family, you might want to try activities like these.

- Try your hand at tie-dying.

- Learn a new language together.

- Cook together.

- Go to an unknown band's concert.

- Try a martial arts class.

- Go camping or biking.

- Experience rock-climbing.

- Volunteer at a local soup kitchen.

Travel Somewhere New

Get your tickets booked and itineraries logged! Think about it: you and your partner have finally scheduled that trip you have been talking about and are going to get away for a week or two. There will be no work, no responsibilities, nothing! Just you and the exciting endeavors that await you while you travel and explore together. The last thing you are probably envisioning is your in-laws crashing the party and joining you, but don't sleep on it!

Traveling together is a wonderful way to nurture your relationship and find common ground. Whether it's an active trip that involves hiking or skiing, simply touring a new city, or even a vacation focusing on rest and relaxation, any of these can be a perfect destination to take your in-laws to with loads of benefits!

Before getting into the benefits, it is important to note that planning a vacation, especially if you, your partner, or your in-laws have different ideas of the best spot to vacation, can be a little stressful. However, if you can find a place that allows each of you to enjoy your favorite things, there is no way to lose! So brainstorm ideas. Get together and plan it with one another before making any concrete plans.

Shared Experiences Make Lasting Memories

Traveling together allows you and your loved ones to share new and exciting experiences and make memories that could very well last a lifetime. Researchers examined the meanings associated with family vacations and found that people typically view vacations as a way to escape everyday life, provide the family with the opportunity for togetherness, and an opportunity to create long-term positive memories.

Better Communication and Decision-Making Skills

Chapter 2 discusses all things communication, but since it's the most crucial aspect of a relationship, there will always be a communication undertone throughout this guide.

As previously mentioned, planning a vacation can sometimes be difficult and stressful, especially if loved ones have different interests. It doesn't just end at the planning stage, either; the challenge can continue even when you're all on the trip. Set yourself up for success by keeping in mind that your first trip with your in-laws will likely be anything other than a breeze. You can plan everything to a T, but in an unfamiliar area, you might be tasked with extra daily excursions whether they are your idea or someone else's.

Not to mention most people don't plan every meal they eat. It's important to remember that every person on the trip with you will have their own list of "must-see" and "must-do" spots, and it's important to articulate what those are as up front as possible. As you and your family work out your itinerary, you will most certainly benefit from the teamwork of deciding on a plan, but you need to be sure to communicate your wishes for the experience clearly and ask others to do the same. Even though this may be stressful at first, make sure you take the time to appreciate the positivity that can come from it. When dealing with multiple personality types, you can become more equipped to communicate and grow your decision-making skills. If successful, the lessons you learn in planning your trip can hopefully be brought back home to facilitate the ease with which you make household decisions or other familial decisions regarding your in-laws.

Escaping Everyday Stressors

Traveling together and removing yourselves from the stress of work and other responsibilities allows you and your family the time to be truly present and focus on one another without any external distractions. This may not be the reality when you get back home, and that's perfectly fine! But it does allow you to nurture your relationship and solidify the connection you all have while away.

Cherish Memories

Most parents love their children. There are, of course, exceptions, but where does that leave our in-laws? It is important to know that not everyone's experience is the same in this. Some in-laws do unequivocally love their sons- and daughters-in-law. Some, however, do not; and some do but with restrictions and conditions attached.

The truth is that no one is perfect, and that includes relationships. Everyone also has a good bit of trauma that they have held on to to some degree throughout their lifetime. However, the important thing is to recognize the good times over the bad. Always breathe positivity. It will fill your lungs full of love and connection. So cherish the good memories. Think about the good things your in-laws have done for you, and hold on to them. Do avoid forgetting the negative; instead, talk it out and communicate your displeasure as you face it. But do remember to cherish the good times.

Create Memory Gifts

Memory gifts are a great, personalized option that is sure to make your in-laws feel good and a great way to memorialize good times with them. If you haven't established a lot of memories with them yet, make sure you're making new ones and think about doing some of these. Types of memory gifts include personalized photo albums, lockets with photographs inside, and picture ornaments. These sorts of memory gifts are amazing when you want to:

- Feel connected to loved ones.

- Have a story piece to remember your loved ones.

- Preserve your memories.

- Keep a memoir of the past to pass on to future generations.

Create a Family Album

According to research, the use of smartphones for taking photos may actually hinder memory retention. It's so easy to get out your phone and take a photo—so easy that its digital copy loses its importance almost instantly as it is stored away in your digital library. Because of this, consider printing out the most cherished memories and photos. These physical prints can truly offer a sense of connection and belonging if you do this with your family.

Before the era of smartphones, capturing moments through photography was a deliberate process, and physical prints were used exclusively. They served as triggers for memory recall, especially as they were organized into albums. With the freedom to capture countless images on your phone, however, there's a tendency to adopt a snap-now-revisit-later approach, which leads to forgetting a lot of them in the process.

If you're an adult in today's world, the allure of relying on smartphones to document family memories amid a busy schedule is more than understandable. However, since there is also a risk of losing digital photos forever, it seems the risk might overrule the rewards with this one, especially if you're relying on it for preserving memories. The failure to regularly visit digital photos diminishes all the benefits attributed to reminiscing through photographs.

The solution isn't to stop capturing family moments altogether or to stop taking them with your phone if that is what makes sense to you. Research simply suggests that it's essential to be more intentional. When you take a photo with your phone, upload it to a printing service so it can be printed the same week. Displaying these physical photos in albums and up on the walls of our homes is where positive benefits come into play. Research suggests that it enhances self-esteem and reinforces familial bonds.

Physical photos allow for an overall tactile experience that digital photographs simply cannot replicate. By going through these physical photos, you're able to recall memories that stimulate emotional connections. Engaging with physical prints through touch and affection can really strengthen your emotional well-being, and relationships if done together

Go through old photos with your in-laws. If you find you don't have a lot of physical photos, try to go through your digital media to see if you can find some to print off. This can be a great memory-building exercise. Don't forget to also go through physical photographs from when your partner was younger. This can create a stronger bond by showing your interest in your partner's past with your in-laws.

Make plans for future photo sessions. While having our phone cameras at our fingertips is great for capturing everyday moments we might otherwise miss, it's important to note that the bigger things may deserve a little more intention. Consider scheduling a family shoot with a professional photographer, and invite your in-laws (and your parents, too, so there are no ill-feelings). You may be surprised to see how much more of the experience you remember when you let someone else take your photos so that you're able to live in the moment.

In this strange time of self-isolation (in the digital age, self-isolation is on the rise), feeling disconnected is, ironically, becoming a thing we all share (crazy, considering we have devices that make "connection" easier than ever). As your family looks for ways to cope in a world that's increasingly looking to technology to stay connected, remember that it may be something from the past that can reignite their sense of belonging. Taking a little stroll down memory lane and going through photo albums is truly a powerful source of emotional connection and peace—two things that are so, so important in life.

Show You Care with Helpful Surprises

We discussed surprises a little previously. They're not only a great way to communicate with someone, but they're also a wonderful way to show your appreciation and your love for someone.

So what sorts of surprises might show your appreciation to someone?

Well, that depends on the dynamic you have with them. Across the board, practical help is typically noted as being one of the best ways to strengthen a bond. This means doing something that needs doing and that the loved one may not have the time, resources, or skills to do.

Does your father-in-law have a workshop that needs to be cleaned out? While he's out (for work or a vacation) try to get some folks together to do a clean-out. Just make sure you're not throwing away things he would have kept! When you're done, make sure everything is organized in a way that would make sense to him. This kind of surprise not only gets the task done but can also bring added relief for your father-in-law by being able to take it off the to-do list.

Another great surprise is to provide beauty or comfort. Flowers that mysteriously appear at your mother-in-law's front door—or even better, on her table, already cut and in a vase and ready to be admired—can really elevate her day. The same thing can be said about comfort. If you know one of your in-laws has had a bad day, go and offer them something to provide some comfort. Offering a cup of tea, some hot chocolate, or even just a nice meal can provide a little satiation and comfort to someone feeling down.

So how do surprises show love and appreciation? Knowing what to surprise someone with is a testament to how much you truly know and understand someone. For a surprise to please someone rather than annoy, it must show your understanding of a desire or need that others may not know. Surprises in and of themselves, if you look at them that way, are quite intimate demonstrations of love and affection, which in turn affirms the closeness you're vying for in all of your relationships.

For example, if your mother-in-law is allergic to flowers, would you have gotten them for her? A jar of jam, a nice card, or a box of chocolates might have been a better choice.

If your father-in-law is really particular about the way his tools are organized, would you risk organizing them if you didn't know how he liked them? You might opt to do something different to surprise him instead.

Doing thoughtful things and surprising people with true thought and care can alter their moods. Introducing an unexpected twist to the mundane can shake someone out of their routine and bring them into the moment. This can have two positive outcomes. Firstly, a sudden burst of positivity can replace any fleeting negative feelings. Secondly, repeated exposure to surprises can gradually alter one's expectations. This is particularly beneficial for those seeking more optimism in their lives. Encountering pleasant surprises can eventually reshape one's reaction to the unexpected, transforming fear or avoidance into curiosity.

Reflecting on this, isn't it fun to know that you have the power to alter your loved one's standards as far as surprises go? Use this technique on your in-laws to show your appreciation for them.

Key Takeaways

Chapter 3 underscores the significance of developing and maintaining an emotional connection with your in-laws by appreciating them for who they are and what your relationship is with them right now. This chapter is all about the significance of appreciating your in-laws for who they are presently rather than who they may become in the future. It highlights the importance of expressing gratitude toward them, fostering strong emotional connections, and cherishing the relationship you currently share.

Expressing gratitude is portrayed as a fundamental aspect of nurturing positive relationships, promoting mutual respect, and fostering a sense of appreciation within the extended family. Research suggests that gratitude not only enhances psychological and emotional well-being but also strengthens interpersonal bonds. Practical ways of expressing gratitude, such as offering random acts of kindness, maintaining respect in interactions, and writing letters of appreciation are discussed as effective methods of cultivating gratitude for your in-laws.

Furthermore, the chapter emphasizes the necessity of nurturing the relationship with your in-laws by embracing forgiveness, practicing compassion, and accepting them for who they are. We learned conflict resolution strategies such as forgiveness and compassion, as they are essential components of healing and strengthening the bonds you have with your family. Accepting and understanding one another helps foster healthy relationships with in-laws, and creating and maintaining traditions together deepens connections and creates lasting memories.

The chapter also suggests more ways to appreciate your in-laws by finding common ground with them. To do this, explore shared interests and engage in new activities together. This will build new memories through shared experiences. These activities include traveling to new destinations, trying new hobbies, and documenting moments through photography. Each of these is presented as a means of strengthening bonds and promoting a sense of togetherness.

Get Real With Your In-Laws

Navigating relationships with in-laws can be rewarding but can also be incredibly challenging. Chapter 4 delves into the intricacies of building genuine connections with your in-laws and emphasizes the importance of being real with them. Do this by getting to know them as people first and foremost and striving to become their friend. This allows you to truly grasp a true understanding of them and what each of you can bring to the table of your relationship.

Here, we'll explore many ways of becoming more authentic with each other, including learning their strengths and becoming their friend. Just as with any developing friendship, we build relationships by showing interest in them, asking their advice, being present, being vulnerable, apologizing when necessary, and addressing tough issues when they arise.

Learn Their Emotional Strengths

Learning about and celebrating the emotional strengths each person brings to the familial table is essential for bonding and growth. To love your in-laws more effectively, it's important to try and resonate with them emotionally.

Take the time to identify and acknowledge the unique emotional strengths each of you has. Introverted people can often bring introspection, empathy, and stability, while more extroverted family members may contribute enthusiasm, spontaneity, and optimism. Recognize how your emotional strengths complement your in-laws individually and vice versa.

For example, there are some people who can provide a stabilizing presence during challenging times. These people are typically more level-headed and patient. If you have an in-law who exhibits this kind of behavior, they may bring great emotional strength in times of distress. On the flip side, there are also people who are really good at being positive and energetic during times when negativity could normally take over. Ultimately, personality strengths are part of people's identity. Your in-laws have them just like everyone else, even if it may not seem like it or you would rather not admit it. Learn to appreciate these differences.

Your in-laws having different emotional strengths than you or your partner is quite a good thing because often the relationships become more stable over time as a result. This is because each of you can feed off the other's energy. Where one person lacks, the others can cover the bill and vice versa. It's important to take a little time to get to know your in-laws individually and identify their strengths. However, keep in mind that although their traits can benefit you through your relationship with you, they are their gifts and their gifts alone. They choose who to bless with those gifts. The most important thing is to get to know them enough to get a feel for the gifts they possess.

Sometimes we aren't able to see our biggest strengths ourselves, and it takes a close friend or relative to point them out. By learning the strengths your in-laws have to offer, you may be able to help

them appreciate themselves more. Be that person for them, and they may even return the favor!

Once they do show these emotional strengths in your relationship, make sure that you often express your gratitude for it. For example, if you've had a particularly bad day and your in-law has supported you and breathed a fresh, upbeat, and optimistic breath of fresh air into your lungs, make sure you acknowledge that and express your gratitude to them. Perhaps you feel like your life has been rolling down a tumultuous road and they bring stability where you don't feel it anywhere else, even with your biological parents. Let them know how their qualities have positively impacted you. A simple "thank you" can go a long way.

Become Their Friend

Friends are important no matter what stage of life you're in. Friends help us when we are in need, they make us feel supported, and they make life much more enjoyable. When finding a friend, what you generally do is gravitate toward people who have interests or hobbies in common with you. This is no different when making your in-laws your friends.

Being someone's friend also means being there for them in times of need. Did their tire go flat? Did they lock themselves out of the house? Did their electricity malfunction or a pipe burst? Be the person that helps them when they need help. If you have the skillset to fix the issue, do it yourself—but if you don't have the skillset, help them by suggesting someone who does or by making that call yourself.

Show Interest in Them as People

A great way to get real with your in-laws is by getting to know them as people. Obviously, if you're trying to become their friend, you have to try to get to know them as people, so taking a step back and showing interest in them, their past, and their future can help you do that. Two ways to do that involve learning about the five love languages and showing interest in their pasts.

The Five Love Languages

Most people in Western culture have heard of *The Five Love Languages*, by Dr. Gary Chapman. It is a book that was written in 1995 and has become incredibly popular. The book paved the way for a new way of thinking. It allowed for greater insight as to how each person shows love and how we like to receive love. The book suggests that everyone has their own "love language" and explains how to show someone that love in a way that they can truly experience it.

A great way to show appreciation to your in-laws is by learning their love language and trying to love them in their own language. Here are Chapman's five love languages. We all use and enjoy every one of them to some extent; this exercise is about becoming aware of each other's strongest preferences rather than identifying only one love language per person.

> **Words of affirmation.** We have all heard it before: "actions speak louder than words," and while this may be true, words can mean just as much as actions for certain people. Positive affirmations are incredibly important, for example, for children during the rearing ages. In fact, positive affirmations have

been shown to increase mental well-being in the same way as nutrition, sleep, and exercise.

Your words of affirmation can give someone who speaks this love language the ability to focus on the positive even in a particularly negative situation. Speak positively to your in-law if you feel this is their love language.

Quality time. This is something that most of us value. In fact, one could argue that most people enjoy quality time in one way or another. If this is someone's primary love language, consider taking your loved one on a family vacation or merely taking them out to a Sunday brunch for a one-on-one meal and conversation time. This could mean watching a movie with someone who is a little more introverted or going out to a big event with someone a little more outgoing. No matter what you do, just make sure you're actively participating and giving them your undivided attention. This is especially true if this is their designated love language.

Giving gifts. Who doesn't like gifts? While some may like more extravagant gifts than others, everyone does enjoy a present from time to time. If this is someone's love language, this is how they prefer love to be shown to them (and may be how they prefer to show love as well).

Gifts can be for special occasions or no reason at all. It doesn't have to be expensive, just thoughtful. If your in-laws enjoy receiving gifts as part of their love language, make sure that you shower them with presents on birthdays and holidays, and don't forget to throw in a random Tuesday in there from time to time!

Physical touch. While this may be a little more difficult with your in-laws depending on your current relationship or your preferences, be aware that this may be at least one of their love languages. If you give everyone in your family a hug during get-togethers and skip your in-laws, it might make them feel rejected or unloved especially if it is one of their primary love languages. Find out if that's something your relationship is missing with your in-laws and work through your own emotions as to how you might go about showing them physical affection. Don't make yourself uncomfortable for the sake of someone else, but don't ignore that this could be an important opportunity to speak your in-law's language for the sake of your relationship.

Acts of service. The final love language is acts of service, which is basically just love in action. If that's your in-laws' love language, then that old saying "actions speak louder than words" rings true one hundred percent in this scenario. This can include driving them somewhere, picking up their dry cleaning, helping them around the house, etc.

No matter what love language your in-laws gravitate toward, learn it and see what you can do to show them that you truly do love and appreciate them for who they are!

Show Interest in Their Past

Another way to show interest in your in-laws' lives is by showing interest in their past. This can be the past that they have with your partner or the past even before your partner was conceived. It's easy to see your in-laws and forget that they had an entire life before you, your spouse, or even each other. We get so caught up in the day-to-day noise of life—the transactional updates and small talk or the habitual avoidance of controversial topics—that we sometimes forget to really get to know our loved ones on a deeper level. If you are looking to get to know your in-laws in a whole new light, strengthen or reset your relationship, or maybe just connect your children to them, having some insight into their past may be a great place to start.

Ask Their Advice

Every parent enjoys giving their children advice. Your in-laws would likely revel at the thought of giving you and your spouse advice, so if you're looking at ways to appreciate them, ask for their help! This will not only aid in your relationship, but it could also give you a little more ammo in your arsenal of appreciation.

While you can set boundaries for your parents and in-laws and vice versa, it's important to note during your boundary discussion the importance of respecting one another's advice as well. For example, if you're going to ask your in-laws for advice, don't ignore them when they give it to you. That shows you don't respect them or their time. Going to them for advice may seem like second nature at this point, but it shouldn't be taken for granted. Or, on the flip side, it may sound absolutely horrifying to you to ask them for advice. In that case, why would you put yourself through a difficult situation only to not listen to or take the advice seriously? Either way, your in-laws will feel important and trusted if you go to them for advice every once in a while, and if they give you that advice, make sure you're taking proper care to heed it—or at the very least, thank them for it if you take a different route.

Most importantly, it's critical to understand that there is nothing ever wrong with asking for help. As much as your pride may tell you that it's terrible to ask for help, it's not. Everyone needs it every now and then, just like everyone needs advice. Remember, those who are successful in life are not those who don't have obstacles; they're the ones who are able to find the resources and tools to make those obstacles disappear.

It's also important to understand that when you do need help, it's important to be the one to bring it up. Pick a low-key moment. Don't make it out to be some big, dramatic thing. It's always easier to talk to someone when everyone feels comfortable and relaxed.

Be expressive and heed some of the advice from Chapter 2 in regard to communicating and expressing your feelings. If you're having an issue with something, make sure that you let your in-laws know what you're feeling. Describe what you're having trouble with and how it is affecting you. If you don't quite know how to communicate it, then tell them, "I'm not sure what I'm feeling, but I don't feel like myself." Maybe even let them know certain symptoms you have and in what way you don't feel like yourself. Maybe you're tired lately; maybe irritable. Or maybe you know exactly what's wrong. Whatever the case, communicate what you can so they can better help you.

Ask for What You Want

It's important to specify if you want help or if you purely want advice. The two are not synonymous with one another, although they can go hand-in-hand. It's important to differentiate between the two to set yourself and the relationship up for success. Don't get caught up trying to analyze or explain the whys, especially when you don't know. If you need help, let your in-laws know what you need and to what extent you feel you need it. Everyone gets nervous or upset sometimes, but let them know if it is more serious than that. They can't read your mind.

At the end of the day, if you want to develop and grow your relationship with your in-laws, it's likely that you care for them and that they care for you. If you do care for them, you have to learn to trust them. Let them know you need help, and let them help you decide what sort of help you need.

Try Again If Need Be

An important note is that if you need to, try again later. Sometimes we can't bring ourselves to tell our loved ones what is wrong. And sometimes when we're ready to talk, who we want to talk to isn't available. And sometimes, frankly, it's just not a good time. If that's the case, don't fret. It's entirely possible that your in-laws just don't have the time at the moment. If you feel as though your in-laws are brushing you off, try again later. Sometimes people just need a little time to understand where you're coming from. If it's necessary, ask them when they may be free to talk, or respectfully confront them and ask why they're dodging you.

Be Present

Get real and be present! In an increasingly technology-driven world, the importance of being fully present with family cannot be overstated. In-laws are no exception to that. It is critical to make a conscious effort to disconnect from the distractions of technology when you can to focus on what truly matters: your relationships. Three steps will aid in this endeavor: put away your phone, limit TV time, and show affection.

Put Away Your Phone

The first step is to put away your phone. Although easier said than done, this is perhaps the most crucial step as it is likely the biggest distraction to a majority of people today. While there's a time and place for technology, it's crucial to learn to prioritize family and relationship connections over your devices. By setting your phone on vibrate and placing it out of reach during family time, you send a clear message to everyone involved that they're your top priority.

Limit TV Time

While TV can be a fun and engaging experience—and a great opportunity for family bonding, if done appropriately—it can also become a default option. When it becomes a default option, it's no longer about family time and more about watching something to ignore one another. By prioritizing a more interactive and engaging activity over passive screen time, you're prioritizing your relationships. Take a walk, visit the park, or enjoy a meal together! Strive to make a meaningful connection with your in-laws while they're still with you.

Show Affection

Expressing love and affection is essential in nurturing strong family bonds, as we have discussed. Whether it's through hugs, kisses, or simple gestures of affection, demonstrating love reinforces the importance of family and strengthens our relationships. As a bonus, showing affection is also a great way to show you are present in the moment.

Share Personal Stories

Telling personal stories is about more than just talking about yourself. It is an ongoing conversation that you have with loved ones that can deepen connections by creating intimacy and allowing for an opportunity to seek support. Sharing things about yourself and learning more about others is what creates lasting relationships. Share some stories about yourself with your in-laws to experience the benefits of this powerful tool.

- **Stronger emotional bonds.** By sharing details about your life, you let your in-laws in on who you are and who their child has chosen as their partner. This can create a bond, which can in turn allow everyone the opportunity to feel seen, heard, and understood.

- **Increased trust.** By sharing details about yourself, especially intimate ones, you're showing your in-laws that you trust them. Likewise, this might allow them the opportunity to trust you and share details about themselves as well.

- **Sense of belonging.** Studies show that human beings crave social interaction and a sense of belonging. By sharing details about yourself, you're opening up and creating a sense of belonging. This is especially true if they feel safe to open up to you as well.

- **Social support.** Disclosing things about yourself is key to forming true support networks. If no one knows you or what your struggles are, how are they ever supposed to support you? By opening up, you allow people to be that for you. It's important to note that having social support in your life can lessen stress and provide substantial emotional validation.

Be Vulnerable

As scary as being vulnerable may feel, it can also be incredibly beneficial. Think about it: if you only share the comfortable and safe parts of yourself, how can your relationship grow?

What makes the relationships you have differ from one another? Being vulnerable with others is known to foster closeness, trust, and intimacy because it tells the person you're with that you trust them. This in turn allows you to truly get to know each other.

Of course, if being vulnerable were easy, we'd do it all the time. The truth is, it can be scary and difficult. If you already feel judged by your in-laws, this may seem like the last thing in the world you'd like to do. Our past traumas can even make being vulnerable even harder. However, despite it being scary, there are small things you can do in order to develop vulnerability in your relationship with your in-laws, no matter what that relationship currently looks like.

Start slow. The biggest thing to all of this is to start slow and small. You don't want to jeopardize your own mental health in an attempt to grow a relationship. Make sure that you gauge your in-laws accurately. Are they the type to be supportive? Do they laugh at, judge, or dismiss your vulnerabilities? By starting small you can evaluate their responses. If they do respond well, then consider sharing again—maybe something a little bigger next time.

Be honest. When you're being vulnerable, it's important to be honest. By sharing your opinion about certain things/ situations without altering it based on how you think they will feel about it, you're being vulnerable. This is critical also in learning how to be yourself.

Express your needs. Our family members aren't mind readers. And that's perfectly okay! When you're being vulnerable with family (especially your in-laws), make sure that you ask for what you need from them. If they don't know what you need from them, it can feel frustrating when your needs aren't met. However, that is an unfair expectation to put on anyone, especially your in-laws. Make sure that you let them what you expect from them when you're being vulnerable. Otherwise, you risk shutting down and harming your relationship when the entire point is to strengthen it and the intimacy between you.

Apologize When Necessary

We've all been hurt before, and we've all wanted someone to apologize to us before. We hope it restores dignity and trust or even provides a sense of justice. But regardless of what we hope, what we expect is an apology that is thoughtful rather than one that is thoughtless. In fact, when an apology is thoughtful and well-intended, it can often mend a relationship (if the offense isn't drastic), but when it's thoughtless, it only incites further conflict.

So, what makes an effective apology? Clearly, thoughtfulness. But what else?

Here are a few criteria for effective apologies.

- Admit to the offense and show your understanding of the error of your behavior.

- Acknowledge that the offense caused harm (the person you're apologizing to might need recognition that their feelings were legitimate).

- Take responsibility. Let them know if it was or was not intentional.

- Include a statement of regret. "I'm sorry" is a necessary part of the apology but falls short of being complete. Tell them why you are sorry.

- Finish with a promise not to repeat the offense and/or an acknowledgment of what you will do differently going forward.

Be Yourself

As much as we might like to think we're authentic beings and we keep it real with everyone we meet, we may come to find that we aren't quite always ourselves. Instead of always being and showing our authentic selves, most people construct personas as a way to look good, please others, or avoid pain, embarrassment, or rejection. Without even meaning to, at times we fashion a "self" that is not wholly us. This is referred to as a *fabricated self*.

Psychologists recommend that humans express what they are experiencing inside. If you are feeling angry or sad, it's important you acknowledge and honor that. This means that rather than flash a fake smile or pretend that you're fine, you have the awareness to be emotionally honest and genuine with yourself and the courage to express it to others.

Authenticity with yourself is easier said than done, of course. It's a quite vulnerable experience to be yourself, especially when what you're feeling is off-putting. However, it's important to note that we cannot enjoy deep and satisfying connections if we're not being emotionally honest with ourselves.

Address Tough Issues

Be open, honest, and calm during conversations with your in-laws. It's all about being real with them. Make sure that you stand your ground and hold fast to your point, but also make sure that you're remaining open to listening to their side of things. If there are issues you really need to discuss, decide what you're going to say beforehand and allow your anger to subside before you speak to them. Here are several other tips to make this opportunity successful.

- **Propose a time and place to talk in person.** While it can be tempting to confront someone through less confrontational means, such as phone calls or via text or email, it should be avoided if at all possible. Talking face-to-face is a much more powerful way to resolve an issue efficiently and effectively. This also presents a lower chance of misconstruing what the other person is saying.

- **Make your point known and keep your composure.** Keep your confrontation calm, composed, and collected. It is usually best to confront someone with a few brief, factual statements. Remember your communication techniques in this confrontation, too. Use neutral language and don't instigate more conflict.

- **Be as open, honest, and direct as possible.** Even if you disagree with your in-laws on a certain issue, it is important for you to be able to attempt a mature conversation. Make sure you're open, honest, and direct without being defensive, cruel, or underhanded. The point is to work through the issue rather than incite a larger one. Reciting what you have prepared will help you present your issue in the best possible way for everyone.

- **Listen to your in-laws.** A productive conversation depends on both parties communicating effectively. This happens through each party contributing and each party listening. By using your active listening skills, you help your in-laws feel respected and heard. Even if you don't agree with what they're saying, allowing them to share their thoughts and listening to them is critical. Don't ever assume you know what they're going to say.

Key Takeaways

This chapter is all about getting real with your in-laws. It discusses the significance of recognizing and celebrating the emotional strengths your in-laws can bring to the table, even ones you might not have known before. By getting to know your in-laws on a personal and friendly level, you're more able to identify the unique attributes each one of them brings to the family. This allows you to truly harbor a deeper sense of appreciation and understanding for one another and the gifts each person can provide. Whether it's providing stability during challenging times or infusing positivity and energy into family dynamics, understanding and valuing these emotional strengths can lead to stronger relationships in general and flow throughout your entire family unit, not just between you and each of your in-laws.

Beyond learning about your in-laws in a way that captures their personality essence and allows for you to grow into being friends, the chapter briefly explores the concept of love languages and suggests learning and catering to the love languages of your in-laws as a way to keep it real, express yourself, and show your love in a way that means the most to them. Whether it's through words of affirmation, quality time, acts of service, gifts, or physical touch, understanding and speaking each of your in-laws' love languages can truly foster deeper connections and bring forth more opportunities for trust and acceptance.

Other great ways the chapter suggests for you to get to know your in-laws and keep it real with them is to show interest in their past. Do this by playing games and getting everyone else involved too. It's important to remember that our in-laws and parents had lives before us. Knowing where they come from and how the version of them you see and know today came to be will help you gain a true understanding of them, which will help you have more compassion for them.

When delving into your in-laws' lives and getting to know them, it is even more important to be completely present and disconnect from distractions. This not only shows your respect for them but also gives you a greater insight into who they are because you are able to actually listen and pay attention.

Other ways to show your love for your in-laws and keep it real include sharing personal stories, being vulnerable, calmly addressing issues when they arise, and engaging in meaningful conversations. All of these can truly nurture your relationship into something incredible and worth working for.

Chapter 5

Family Fun

No matter what your family dynamic looks like, a little family fun can help create and maintain a genuine connection with your loved ones. Chapter 5 delves into how to take this family fun and turn it into more ways to love your in-laws. The chapter will explore various avenues that strengthen your bonds with your in-laws and simultaneously create lasting memories. From surprising visits to engaging in laughter-filled activities, this chapter is a guide to not only bridge the gap between you and your in-laws but also to truly nurture a meaningful relationship with them built on laughter, shared experiences, and inclusivity.

Invite them Over

Don't just invite them over for game nights; invite in-laws over for dinners, or just because, too! Having family over, especially your in-laws, may seem daunting. If this isn't you, then congratulations. However, if the idea of family get-togethers seems daunting, intimidating, or even just downright awful, start with a little organization. With some creativity and planning, you can throw a stress-free family get-together. This can be anything from a family reunion to a block party or holiday event.

If you're hoping to grow your relationship with your in-laws, make sure you include them. This can be with both sides of your family or just your in-laws. Remember, you're not choosing over family members; you're just planning a get-together. Just be sure that the next get-together goes to the other side of the family.

When deciding on a family get-together, think about your invitees, place and time, and specifics such as food (will this be over a meal time, or are snacks more appropriate?). After you plan all this out, you will have a much easier time planning the rest.

If there is a specific event or get-together that your in-laws do together, consider taking this over for them for the year (or indefinitely if they're getting older and having a difficult time continuing the tradition). It can really alleviate some stress for them and give you a chance to toss your creative flair into the mix and also create new, refreshing family memories.

Remember, planning is the key to organizing a successful family get-together. Work with your in-laws to determine who to invite, time and place, and food. It may seem obvious to you who to invite, but if you (or they, more specifically) have a large family, the guest list could become overwhelming, especially if you aren't used to hosting. Also, make sure you get their input and expertise on a few traditions. Ask which you should refresh and which you should keep the same. The idea isn't to step on any toes; it's to help and make it an enjoyable experience. By getting their input, you're showing that you value them just as much as you do your family fun.

No matter how simple or grand the party is, hosting a family get-together is hard work that can give you, your partner, and your in-laws an amazing bonding experience.

Include Them

Have you ever felt isolated or that you just didn't belong? How would you feel if it was your family unit where you felt you didn't belong?

Remember that being truly inclusive is ensuring everyone is invited to that barbeque or that everyone participates in the family Christmas name drawing. Human beings are social creatures; Inclusion fosters a sense of belonging and provides safety and recognition in groups. At our core, we are animals, and as such, we innately crave this sense of belonging and desire to be part of a community or group.

Studies have shown that without this feeling of belonging, people feel threatened and pressured to expend energy by pretending to be someone they're not. This can have detrimental effects on mental well-being, leading individuals to doubt the worthiness of others' time. Certainly, no one would wish for anyone to experience such emotions. If you're reading this guide, it's likely because you value creating environments where people feel psychologically secure and valued, especially those you love. Creating such an atmosphere encourages openness and understanding, allowing for genuine connections without hasty judgments or assumptions. So please, include your in-laws!

Have Family Outings

Adults and children alike benefit from spending quality family time together. Children feel special when their parents take the time to do fun activities with them; even simple everyday errands can make for great bonding experiences. This is also true of their grandparents. If you have children, your children benefit from seeing you spending time with their grandparents and for all of you to be spending time with them. Likewise, your partner would likely like to see all of you doing things together from time-to-time too. Here are just a few ways that family outings benefit everyone.

- Creating a stronger emotional bond between family members.

- Allowing for better communication between family members.

- Superior performances in school and work for children and adults.

- Children are less likely to exhibit behavioral problems.

Work and extracurricular activities (whether those are for you or your children) can make for very busy schedules without a lot of extra room for family activities. If this is your family, that's okay! Simple things like having dinner together at a restaurant on a scheduled night every month can have an impact as well.

If you do have a little more time to set aside, just know that spending quality time doesn't have to cost a lot of money, either. In fact, some of the most fun activities are little-to-no-cost adventures.

- **Volunteer.** As we discussed earlier in things you can do with your in-laws, don't sleep on volunteering together! This can involve the entire family for a little fun. Instill a sense of empathy in your children, too, by getting them involved. This will give them the family time they crave and help them learn positive ways to give back.

- **Visit a fire or police station.** Schedule a tour with your local fire department or at the police station in your town. Children will have a great time meeting the firemen or police officers and getting a behind-the-scenes tour of where they work. And they may be able to see the vehicles! This is a great outing to do with your in-laws because it's interactive and your in-laws can get a good educational experience with their grandchildren.

- **Go to the zoo or aquarium.** This is a great family outing for all ages. Not only is it fun to see and interact with animals you may not see in your day-to-day but it's also a great way to exercise and get those steps in! Zoos and aquariums are amazing outings to do with your in-laws and something they are sure to enjoy, especially if it gives them time with their grandchildren and adult child.

- **Go to a minor-league game.** Have a fun night out at the ballpark. Hot dogs, pretzels, and charged crowds are a great way to spend time together. Cheer on your local minor-league team and enjoy the camaraderie of one another. It's typically easy to get tickets to a minor league game and a much more affordable option for families on a budget.

- **Sample exotic cuisine:** Calling all foodies! While you may have a picky eater on your hands (especially if you have children), everyone generally enjoys food. Find a type of food that your children and in-laws have yet to sample and find a restaurant that serves it. Make it a game and have fun taste-testing different dishes with them to see what everyone can agree on.

Create Family Game Nights

Just like going on family outings, family game nights are a great way to interact with your in-laws and include them in family fun. When you sit down to play a game with your family, you are building relationships, making space for important conversations, practicing all-important social skills, working on brain and strategy skills, and, probably most importantly, you're making memories.

If game nights have always been a part of your family's culture, it may not seem like that hundredth run of Monopoly is important, but it is. You are building something larger, something that you can't see right now, but it exists! It's also necessary to help your in-laws feel welcome (whether you had game nights as a child or not). Continually including them will solidify your relationships, so play! Enjoy each other. Make memories. Remember that just because you plan game nights with one set of parents (your in-laws, in this case) doesn't mean you can't do the same with the other set of parents (your parents, in this case). Experiment with times that work for everyone. If you can't do two game nights a week, a month, etc., consider alternating to every-other to make time for everyone; or consider a mega-gathering!

Here's a quick and easy guide to incorporating successful game nights into your family culture.

- **Schedule a time that works for everyone.** The term "family game night" means the family is involved, but it doesn't have to happen in the evening. Schedule a time that works best for you and your family. Whenever there's downtime, you should schedule your game time. Just make sure you set a day and a time that works for all members of your family, and then try to stick to it. Consistency will mean the most in this. If a weekly game night is too overwhelming, try something monthly first (and as mentioned earlier, if you're alternating with other family members, do it every other month). It's not supposed to feel like a chore, but it should require a bit of sacrifice. It doesn't matter when or how often; just you pick something that can work so you can stick to it.

- **Pick more than one game.** Have a few games in mind for any given night. Some families have a few favorites they want to play every time. Others keep a rotation of a few tried and true games but keep it fun and fresh with a few curveballs from time to time. And then some families may prefer a new game every single time. Consider rotating who picks the game or brings it, or set up a subscription that sends new games every month. Whatever you decide, make sure everyone is on board and it's appropriate and easy enough for everyone intended to play.

- **Do not disturb.** Make a ritual out of setting your phones to Do Not Disturb mode. Having technology at your fingertips is wonderful, but you don't need it for game night—unless you choose to incorporate video games into your game nights. Turn off televisions and other distractions as well. This is a time for family!

- **Make sure there's food.** Everyone loves food. Everyone loves drinks. Make sure that you have plenty planned, whether it's takeout, something you cook, or potluck. Every time there's a game night planned, make sure food is involved.

- **Remember to have fun.** It's easy to get wrapped up in everyday life. It's even easier to let it affect your mood when you spend time with your family. But don't let it! This is a time for you and yours, so enjoy each other and remember that real life will be there when you're finished with your time together. Game nights should be fun and stress-free, even if the game itself is new and challenging. Try to relax. Be mindful of the moment and know that you're creating memories that can last a lifetime!

- **Be patient.** If you're the type to be overly competitive, make sure you're being patient with those who may need a bit more time to understand the game. Be patient with children who may argue; just explain to them calmly that it's a game and that you're all learning and trying to have fun together. Understand that all game nights won't be perfect, and don't let your expectations ruin the good nature of the evening. Kids will argue. Tears may even happen for more sensitive family members. Accusations of cheating may flow. There may also be sore winners and sore losers. Whatever the case, just remember that you and your family are together and you're playing. And use these times as teachable moments for you and your family and discuss ways to improve.

- **Thank everyone for coming.** This may sound silly, but when everyone is finished playing, thank them. Thank your in-laws for coming, thank them for playing, and thank them for interacting with one another. Tell them you had fun playing with them and that you're looking forward to the next time.

- **Plan the next one.** Even if you have the same day and time in place for every game night, make sure you plan the next one. This can be as simple as confirming everyone will be there at the day and time agreed upon or asking what you're having for dinner that night. Just make sure that you plan it and that everyone has it locked into their calendars so they don't forget.

Plan a Surprise Visit

We discussed surprises before, but what better way to be real with your in-laws than taking a trip to visit them? Or better yet, plan a surprise visit to one of their favorite venues (zoo, aquarium, amusement park) with them.

Make Them Laugh

Think about it: not everyone can make you laugh. That's something only a few select people can do in your life. It's likely the case with your in-laws too. Be someone that makes them laugh—and laugh with them!

Laughter releases endorphins. Endorphins are peptides that activate our body's opiate receptors. In layman's terms, endorphins make you feel good about yourself and others. These sorts of feelings can create a bond between people and allow for a tighter sense of togetherness. Remember, the goal is to become friends with your in-laws, too. And the golden rule of friendship is that if you make people feel good about themselves (and you), they will like you! Laughter is one of the best ways to do that.

Key Takeaways

Chapter 5 emphasizes the importance of actively engaging with your in-laws through enjoyable activities and shared experiences. It stresses the importance of inclusivity and belonging within the family unit, encouraging readers to create environments where all members feel valued and included.

The chapter explores the benefits of family outings, outlining the positive impact it has on familial bonds, communication, and your overall well-being. Suggestions for family outings include volunteering, visiting local attractions like fire or police stations, exploring zoos or aquariums, and attending minor league games.

Additionally, the concept of family game nights as an opportunity for interaction, communication, and memory-making is also an astounding way to have fun and connect. Practical tips for organizing successful game nights include thoughtful scheduling, game selection, and minimizing distractions.

The chapter advocates surprise visits as a means of fostering authenticity and connection. It highlights the significance of laughter in building bonds and suggests incorporating humor into interactions with in-laws because laughter is seen as one of the best ways to make others feel good about themselves and you.

Supporting Your In-Laws

In this chapter, we delve into the crucial aspect of supporting your in-laws while recognizing the significance of developing and maintaining strong relationships. In order to achieve this, we must be willing to offer support and assistance in various facets of their lives. From practical help around the house to navigating the digital landscape, offering emotional support during challenging times, and addressing financial concerns, this chapter offers valuable insights and strategies to enhance your connection with your in-laws and navigate familial dynamics effectively in a supportive and caring way. Whether it's lending a helping hand with chores, serving as a tech guru, offering a listening ear, or providing financial assistance, each form of support contributes to building trust, strengthening bonds, and fostering a sense of unity within the family. Through thoughtful guidance and practical advice, this chapter aims to empower readers to navigate the complexities of supporting their in-laws with compassion, understanding, and resilience.

Offer to Help with Chores

Let's face it, no one is getting any younger, and everyone needs a little help now and then. Your in-laws are no exception to this rule.

It's important to show your in-laws that you're appreciative of them and that you care enough to want to help them. Offering to help your in-laws and loved ones with chores around the house and yard is one of the best ways to show your support to them.

Around the House

Whether or not they still have children in the house, your parents and in-laws are still working hard running their home and possibly maintaining their jobs. Additionally, they may be facing challenging involved in aging.

You can show your in-laws how much you appreciate them by helping out with chores around the house when you have extra time on your hands (or even better, prioritize the time to help them). Ask them what you can do to help them if you're not sure where you might be most needed. They will likely appreciate your thoughtfulness!

If your partner's family has a dog, a cat, a bird, a fish, or any animal that eats—or if they got it after your partner left the nest— offer to help take care of them when your family is hanging out around the house or visiting. You could also be a huge help and take the pet out for a walk, play fetch, or play with them with other toys.

Here are more chores you, your partner, or your children can do to help your in-laws around the house.

- Taking out the trash

- Doing the laundry

- Dusting unused areas

- Cleaning floors

- Helping with dinner

- Washing dishes

- Organizing those boxes in the garage

- Helping out with a particular skillset you may have, such as electrical work or carpentry.

In the Yard

Yardwork is one of those chores most of us really need help with the older we get. Not only is it physically taxing, but the heat in the summer can be very dangerous to an older person. Grab a watering can and give your in-laws' thirsty plants a drink, whether indoors or out. Remember that plants only need to be watered at certain times—if you don't know how to properly care for their plants, ask them! You never want to turn good-natured help into an inconvenience.

Pull weeds for them, do some landscaping, or pressure-wash their drive. The sky is the limit, and they will likely appreciate any help you can give. Remember, if it's something you would help your parents with, help your in-laws with it.

Singular Favors

Run errands for them from time to time, and if you're out and about and going to be near their neighborhood, call and ask them if they need anything.

And if your partner does have younger siblings or stepsiblings, offer to watch them from time to time so your in-laws can go out and do whatever they'd like.

Act as Tech Support

Navigating the digital landscape can be a daunting task for anyone, especially for our older family members. As you seek to strengthen your bond with your in-laws, providing tech support can serve as a powerful bridge and help them rely on you. Here's how you can become their go-to tech guru while fostering a deeper connection and developing a richer trust.

- **Identify their specific needs.** Begin by understanding their specific tech challenges. Are they struggling with setting up email accounts, navigating social media platforms, or managing their devices? Take note of their pain points to tailor your support accordingly.

- **Having patience is key.** Remember, patience is crucial when assisting older adults with technology. Approach each session with empathy and understanding. Avoid rushing or displaying frustration when they don't get it right away, as this could discourage them from seeking your help in the future. The goal is to get them to trust you, not for them to feel judged, made fun of, or as if they're burdens.

- **Empower them to fix their own issues.** Instead of simply fixing their tech issues, empower your in-laws to troubleshoot problems independently. Teach them basic troubleshooting techniques and provide simple, step-by-step instructions they can refer to in the future. The Chinese philosopher Lao Tzu once said, "Give a man a fish and you feed him for a day. Teach him how to fish and you feed him for a lifetime."

- **Encourage them to learn.** Encourage your in-laws to embrace learning opportunities, whether through online tutorials, community classes, or tech workshops. Offer to go with them to these sessions or provide recommendations.

- **Stay updated.** Keep up to date on the latest technological advancements and trends to better support your in-laws. Introduce them to new tools and applications that could simplify their daily routines or enhance their quality of life.

Remember, they're coming to you. Strengthen the bond and be supportive of them where they need it.

Be Emotionally Supportive

Providing emotional support is a crucial way to help others feel connected and less isolated, especially in challenging times. However, it's important to recognize that being emotionally supportive isn't always straightforward; different situations require different approaches.

Emotional support involves listening without judgment and responding empathetically to someone's feelings and experiences. This may mean resisting the urge to immediately offer solutions or even dismiss their emotions entirely. Studies show that more than half of individuals require emotional support when facing difficult decisions, and for those dealing with mental or physical health issues, having the right support system can significantly enhance their quality of life and even extend it.

So what does effective emotional support entail and what does it have to do with your in-laws? No matter how much it may seem like your in-laws have it together, they might surprise you.

Truth is, everyone needs a little help now and then in the emotional department. You must demonstrate care and compassion through both verbal and nonverbal means and support your in-laws emotionally in any way you can.

Whether it's assisting your in-laws in reaching out to a therapist or offering a comforting embrace to them if they're in distress, emotional support can help them navigate their emotions and remind them that they're not alone. This can ultimately improve their overall well-being and happiness. Doing this also can improve your relationship with your spouse. If they see that you're helping their parents, they will likely feel honored and appreciated as your partner.

Several qualities define good emotional support regardless of the situation or cultural norms involved. However, it should always be respectful, nonjudgmental, compassionate, unconditional, and person-centered. Think about your in-laws individually and who they are. Support them emotionally by truly being there for them as a listening ear.

This is where your active listening skills come in, as they are a key component in showing support. Active listening involves giving undivided attention, allowing them to express themselves freely, asking clarifying questions, and summarizing their thoughts and feelings when they're finished to show them you have been listening and are interested in what they have to say. Here are other techniques of emotional support.

- Empathy. By empathizing with your in-laws' experiences and validating their feelings, you are showing them essential emotional support. Whether acknowledging their anger during a period of grief or expressing understanding for frustrations they may have at work, it's important to validate their emotions and provide comfort and reassurance. This is easier to do when you can understand where they're coming from. Level with them as deeply as you can and put yourself in their shoes.

- Offer love. This may seem like a no-brainer, but offering love and care is enough to make a significant difference in anyone's life, even your in-laws'. It is also essential to show emotional support.

- Offer encouragement. Encourage your in-laws to talk to you and to do things that you know will benefit them. Taking on a new challenge or overcoming an old one is always a struggle. If your in-laws are struggling, it may feel a little odd being someone who is there to support them. It may almost feel like the shoe is on the wrong foot, that you're supposed to be going to them and not vice versa. This means that finding the right words to help can also be difficult. Let them vent and focus on words of positivity and motivation. Use phrases such as:

  ○ You've got this. I believe in you.

  ○ You're not in this alone.

  ○ You can absolutely do this.

  ○ I know it's hard right now, but it's worth doing. Believe in yourself.

  ○ You deserve this opportunity. You're ready for this.

Don't offer unsolicited or rushed advice. It's important not to rush in with judgments or conclusions. It's also important not to rush in with unsolicited advice before you allow them to finish. Let your in-law(s) process their emotions at their own pace.

Offer Financial Help if Needed

If your in-law is struggling financially, you can provide monetary support if you have it. But if you don't have the funds yourself, you can also offer non-monetary support to help improve their situation. Before you write them a check or even offer your advice, though, evaluate their needs and your capacity to meet them so you know what you can offer.

Before your in-law retires or faces serious financial hardship, have an honest discussion with them about the challenges they're having (or expect to have) and the type and extent of help they need or may need in the future. You can help them with their finances in various ways, whether that be through monetary or non-monetary support such as financial advice. The right approach will depend on where everyone is financially—you and them—and where everyone wants to be. Connecting them to a trusted financial advisor can also help facilitate these sorts of conversations.

If they are the types to have diligently saved, budgeted well, are on track to cover their day-to-day expenses, and expect to travel in retirement, their challenge might be having difficulty saving in retirement. In this situation, non-monetary help might be sufficient for their needs; you might help them work out a budget plan to see what they can afford or refer them to a financial professional for more specific advice.

On the flip side, if they are struggling financially in the short term, whether they have unpaid debts, have lost their job, or had to take an early retirement, they may not be able to make ends meet now, let alone have a comfortable retirement in the future. They might prefer monetary support in this scenario, in which case it's useful to inquire about the amount they would need and what their plan would be long-term. Helping them in this situation, both financially and with advice, is crucial. If you don't have the funds to help them, consider other options.

Helping Them Without Providing Money

Not having the money to help your in-laws can be heartbreaking, but there are several ways to support them without opening your wallet.

- **Help them downsize.** If your in-laws are finding their current home unaffordable and there is wiggle room in the size of their home, it may make sense for them to downsize. To determine if it's worth it, help them run the numbers on how much it might save to move to a smaller home. Make sure to factor in not only their mortgage and expenses but the cost of the move as well.

- **Guide them through relocation.** Your in-law may be living in a location with high property taxes. It's entirely possible that they moved there when you were a kid for the schools, and there is no reason for them to stay in that particular area anymore. Help them determine if there's an area better suited for them with a lower cost of living.

- **Ask them to move in.** If they can't afford to live independently, assess their health, your current lifestyle, and the other members of your household to determine whether they can live with you. Taking them in can have a profound positive impact on their finances, often freeing them from a mortgage, rental payments, and associated bills. However, make sure your partner and/or children are comfortable with this, as it can also create chaos if not done properly. This can also impede your own parent's plans if they had ever planned on moving in with you in their old age. So if you do move your in-laws in, this is a discussion best held with both sides of the family.

- **Create a budget for them.** Your in-laws may be seeking ways to stretch their money. This could be to have more money in savings or because they're struggling. Either way, one of the best ways to help them financially is to sit down and draft a basic budget that factors in their income and expenses every month.

- **Help with maintenance or repairs.** If your in-laws need help paying for car or home repairs, and you have the skills to do them, offer to do these repairs for them occasionally.

Providing Care

Is it harder to care for your in-laws or your own parents? It really is a toss-up. That obviously depends on your dynamic. Some women would say their mothers-in-law are absolute nightmares while others absolutely adore their in-laws and have more difficulty with their own parents. Regardless, caregiving is a lot of work no matter which way you slice it. It's important to unpack your emotions with your partner, discuss plans for when both sets of parents are older, and keep an open forum with everyone involved so you can truly develop your family unit in a way that makes sense for everyone and allows for everyone to thrive.

The Impact of Caregiving

Providing financial assistance or physical caregiving to relatives can create strain on the marital relationship. You may have less time to spend together, less money available for pleasure spending, and feel emotionally and physically drained.

Ensure that you're being communicative with your partner on the best ways to provide care for your in-laws. However, don't avoid caring for your spouse's parents. If they want to support their family, it makes sense. That's their family, and they likely made that choice before you were even in the picture, whether they realize it or not. In fact, professionals note that a spouse who doesn't support a partner's caregiving efforts or wishes, takes their relationship with that parent for granted, or doesn't pitch in enough finds themselves headed toward a rocky road in their marriage.

Communication with your partner is essential both before and during caregiving stages. Because even if you want to help your in-laws, do care about your spouse's parent/child relationship, and pull your full weight, it's still a complicated venture—especially if you don't get along with your in-laws.

Some Relationships Are Especially Difficult

Although it's not entirely a shock to most of us, the dynamic you have with your in-laws can be incredibly charged. In fact, according to studies, the mother-in-law/daughter-in-law dynamic is the most charged. If you fall into this category, it may be an even more stressful experience. In fact, statistics show that more than sixty percent of married women felt stress around their mother-in-law as compared to only fifteen percent of men.

Strategies for Caring for Your In-Laws

Going into caregiving for either side of the family, the biggest asset you have is working as a team. Consider these tips as you consider or prepare to take on this big step.

- **Work as a team with your partner.** As stated above, the biggest strategy is to share the load as much as possible. It's even more critical not to adopt a their-parent-not-mine mindset. Making your partner carry the caregiving load all alone can cause anger, resentment, and even depression. Talk about what you need from your spouse and ask them to do the same. Make sure that you're both on the same page. Make sure you express what you are and are not okay with and discuss logistics thoroughly.

- **Express appreciation.** Let your partner know how grateful you are to them, even if it's their parents you're taking care of. However, especially express that appreciation if your spouse is helping you take care of your parents. If your partner took your dad to a doctor's appointment, ran errands for them, or picked up your mom's groceries, for example, let them know how helpful they are and how much what they're doing means to you.

- **Stay emotionally available to each other.** Make sure that you're also being as emotionally available as possible to listen when your partner needs to vent and ask clearly for the same gift when you need it.

- **Don't let others off the hook.** Remember that your life matters. If you are doing most of the work with your parents or your in-laws, make sure that you hold others, such as your siblings or siblings-in-law, accountable for their part.

- **Know your limits.** The most important thing beyond speaking to your partner is knowing the boundaries of what you can do and what you cannot do. Assess this with your partner. Make a list of all of your responsibilities. Understand all of your in-laws' needs. Understand others' expectations and availability, too. What can others do? Is anyone else helping you and your partner care for them? Discuss with your spouse and their family who is "on duty" and when. Don't forget that circumstances may change or tasks may be different or more difficult than you expected or planned for. Have ongoing conversations about how the arrangement is going, and tweak it if you need to. Also, remember that certain jobs can get awkward. Your mother-in-law probably wouldn't want her son to help her bathe or dress, for example, and likewise, a father may prefer his son-in-law rather than his daughter to help him with more intimate care. Discuss these tasks and who should handle them. If you feel uncomfortable performing hygiene tasks with your in-law, for example, it may be worth hiring help so you don't have to do it. Decide what is off-limits and who is going to fulfill those duties.

- **Create a Plan B.** You and your partner will need breaks, and emergencies will arise. Have a backup plan for emergencies and provide regular breaks for the two of you.

- **Consider your in-laws' perspective.** Understand that even if it's frustrating, overly demanding, or awkward for you, it is probably not overly blissful for them either. Most people don't want to admit that they need help or feel like a burden to anyone else, particularly their family members. They might even feel scared, angry, frustrated, depressed, helpless, in pain, or as though their entire world is out of control. They are needing care from someone for the first time since they were children. While it is necessary to keep their feelings in mind, it is also important to remember that toxicity is never to be tolerated. If they're abusive, rude, or unreasonable, make sure that you're having that conversation with them so you can all work through it together.

- **Have realistic expectations.** If you don't enjoy caring for in-laws, there's no reason to feel guilty about that. No one wants to be inconvenienced, and no matter how you spin it, caring for anyone else can be tiresomeness at times. It doesn't matter how much you love your in-laws; the arrangement won't be an easy one. It will take constant effort and communication. If you're the type to pray, those prayers might be super helpful, too. The truth of the matter is things can blow up at any given minute. Emotions run high in situations such as caregiving. Understanding, insight, patience, and a whole lot of time is essential. Going into this with realistic expectations will set everyone up for success. Understand that when it's your in-laws or your parents, your role can be even more demanding than if you were caring for some random elderly person.

Key Takeaways

In this chapter, we focus on providing support to your in-laws in all the various aspects of their lives. It begins with the importance of offering practical help around the house, such as assisting with chores, yard work, and running errands. This type of support demonstrates appreciation and care for your in-laws in everyday situations.

We moved onto other ways to aid our in-laws, including tech support, highlighting the importance of identifying specific tech challenges, exercising patience, empowering them to troubleshoot independently, simplifying complex concepts, and encouraging ongoing learning opportunities. Teach them to fish, don't give them the fish.

Providing emotional support to loved ones is crucial during challenging times. It emphasizes the need for active listening, empathy, validation of emotions, and offering love, care, and encouragement. Emotional support plays a crucial role in improving overall well-being and fostering stronger connections within the family.

Financial support is a challenging topic. We discussed having open discussions about your in-laws' financial challenges and needs and the importance of considering various forms of support, such as monetary assistance or non-monetary support like budget planning or downsizing.

Lastly, the chapter addresses the complexities of caregiving for in-laws, including the dynamics involved and strategies for managing caregiving responsibilities effectively. It emphasizes the importance of teamwork with your partner, expressing appreciation to your partner, involving other family members in the tasks, setting appropriate boundaries and limits, understanding your in-laws' perspective, and acknowledging the challenges involved from their perspective as well as your own.

Celebrate Good Times

Celebrating moments together strengthens familial bonds and creates lasting memories. From honoring traditional holidays to embracing new experiences, Chapter 7 explores various ways to celebrate with your in-laws. Whether it's recognizing milestones, sharing life-altering moments, or traveling together, these activities foster connection and deepen relationships.

Remember Them On (or Around) Father's Day and Mother's Day

This can be a difficult thing, especially when you try to accommodate everyone (including your parents and you and your partner (if you also have kids). Remember, just because you need to remember your in-laws on these holidays doesn't mean it has to be grand or extravagant. It also doesn't have to be immediate. You can give yourself time and space to come up with what works best for you and your family. The truth is, all families look different from the next. Everyone's experience is different. Do what works best for your family.

Celebrate Holidays Together

It's important to find ways to celebrate holidays or create your own family traditions. It's an opportunity to bond and strengthen relationships and a great opportunity to invite your in-laws to join in on the fun and traditions that the holidays offer. In fact, holidays offer the perfect occasion for family reunions; they are opportunities to celebrate the bonds you share with your parents as well as your in-laws. Whether it's the traditional holidays like Thanksgiving, Christmas, or New Year's or even more unique family celebrations, coming together during these special moments strengthens your familial ties and is essential for continued growth and connection.

As families age, sometimes people can start to move away or drift apart. As the family tree branches out, it may be difficult to get together on the bigger holidays. However, by creating or even just revamping your family traditions and rituals, you can still figure out ways to get together. In fact, making this a project with your parents can be a unique way to bond with them. For instance, you might establish an annual family picnic or a family day where you engage in various activities together. These don't have to be near or on big holidays. Many families choose to do these sorts of events on nice warm-weather days that can get the kids outside playing and give the adults a chance to soak in some Vitamin D and enjoy time together. This may be difficult to plan weather-wise if you want it to be on the same day annually, but choose a time when the weather is generally mild, and have both indoor and outdoor activities in mind.

These traditions build a sense of togetherness and make your relationships with your entire family feel more special and distinctive.

Additionally, just taking the time to prepare and enjoy meals together during the holidays or family events can be a deeply bonding experience. Cooking together, sharing recipes, and savoring all of the dishes you've prepared together can create cherished memories for many years to come.

Maintain Old Traditions

Whether these are old traditions of yours that you choose to share with your in-laws or traditions you know your spouse had when they were a child (therefore, old traditions of your in-laws) it's important to incorporate old traditions.

Invite them to Partake in New Traditions

Now that the dynamic of the family has changed (from them spending their holiday celebrations with their child to now spending it with their adult child and that family) it may be a good time to participate in some new traditions.

Moreover, it may be a great opportunity to create traditions. Work together to find things that everyone might enjoy and create your own from scratch! Just make sure that you're being open and accommodating, and that all of you are consistent in making these traditions true to your family.

You and your family likely have your own traditions. It is also possible that your in-laws may not have those same traditions (or religion). If they don't, consider allowing them to bring their own traditions to the celebration and fuse them with yours to create a more harmonious and cohesive family unit.

Invite them to Your House for Dinner

Dinner is a great excuse to come over to the house to celebrate a fun and enjoyable evening. Your in-laws aren't mysterious creatures in the sense that they don't eat! They have to eat. Invite them both over for dinner at your place, whether it's just you or you have a family. This is a great opportunity to let them into your (and their adult child/your partner) world as an adult.

Let Them Bring Something

If they ask what to bring, don't tell them "nothing." Have them bring something! Ask them to bring an appetizer or even a family-favorite dessert if they are up to it. Contributing to the meal might really make them feel special and if they bring something that resonates positively for them and their traditions, it may make it even more special. However, if they're a bit older and have difficulty in the kitchen, maybe ask if they could bring a bottle of wine or a beverage.

Get Them a Ride

Sometimes as your parents and in-laws age, it's difficult to get them to visit. This could be due to a multitude of factors, but for many, the older our family members get, the less likely they are comfortable driving far or at night. Services such as Uber or Lyft (or even a run-of-the-mill taxi company) can make the task a lot more simple. You and/or your partner no longer have to worry about them getting to you, which can mean more time to prepare your meal!

Choose a Meal That Is Tasty but Recognizable

Ask your in-laws over and ask them if there's something they might want or what they would like to bring. If they want to bring a side dish that's specific, think of a meal that might go well with that dish. The goal is to be accommodating to them, their traditions, and their tastes as well as to implement some of your family's favorite traditions or dishes. This is all about inclusion and cohesiveness. You want to fuse as many of each other's traditions as possible. You never know, you may end up finding a new favorite meal.

Keep in mind that older generations also have their favorite dishes and are generally less flexible, so beware of deviating too much from that. If you're looking for a healthy dish, choose one of your parents' favorites but substitute a couple of healthy ingredients. For example, consider ground turkey instead of ground beef or Greek yogurt for cream. These small swaps won't jeopardize the taste of pickier in-laws who may be used to the original dishes and can also be what you and your family need for your appetites.

Let Them Enjoy Your Children

Depending on the dynamic between you and your in-laws, this can be a touchy subject for some families. Obviously, this guide is not a one-size-fits-all. But if you're looking at expanding your relationship with your in-laws and you have children, obviously letting your kids call them Grandma or Grandpa (or a derivative of those terms of endearment) is a great way to start, even if you had your children before marrying your partner (your in-laws' child). Ultimately, if your in-laws have been in the picture, let your kids and the in-laws choose what they are to be called. If your children are comfortable and having fun, let them call them by those sorts of names, and let them experience life together. If your children have been raised with your in-laws participating actively in their lives, make sure they're able to experience bonding separately from you and your spouse.

This is not only a way to show your love for your in-laws but also for your children.

The fact is that family is a treasured gift. Everyone wants their children to trust them and believe that their family members are people who will always be there and who will always love and support one another no matter what. We want them to believe that family comes first. Not just your biological one, either, but all the people you deem as your family.

Remember that your in-laws may not be related to you in a traditional sense, but they are related to your children (unless, of course, you had your children before you were married to their child, and in that case, let your child decide who is family and who isn't).

The biggest gift to a child is to learn that by reaching out to family, they will never be alone. In fact, it's important to encourage your children's familial relationships so they have more than just you and your partner. People who visit them in the hospital when they're getting their tonsils removed, send them birthday cards, come to their games or recitals—these people matter to them. Encourage family members to participate in every aspect of your child's life so they experience these sorts of bonds.

The biggest thing to remember is that your in-laws are not your children's in-laws. Whatever your relationship is with your in-laws doesn't define your child's relationship with them. Your in-laws are your children's family, and they will be forever. Treat them the way you would want your son or daughter-in-law to treat you one day. It is almost guaranteed that you will be glad that you did.

Celebrate Their Anniversary

Without your in-laws, you wouldn't have your partner. Make sure you take the time to celebrate their anniversary because it is an event worth celebrating, no matter what you feel for your in-laws. The truth of the matter is that you have your partner because of their anniversary. However, by celebrating this day and featuring your in-laws, you grow closer to them. This is because you're able to show your appreciation and admiration for your family, where it came from, and where it is going from here. Your in-laws are a huge part of that. Embracing that fact and honoring them and their union is essential.

Travel Abroad With Them

After you've learned to appreciate your in-laws through travel and the lessons you can learn from it, it may be time to travel with them abroad to truly celebrate the relationship to its core.

Traveling with any member of your family, especially your in-laws, may not be the easiest journey to take, but it may be a wonderful way to strengthen and grow your bonds and celebrate the family you and your partner have created together.

Difficulties May Arise

Of course, traveling with extended family is never a simple feat. For one, if there's animosity anywhere in the family, or if your parents feel jealous that you're taking your in-laws rather than them on your vacation, it could make you feel like you're stuck in the middle. Choosing who to go on vacation with may be difficult. However, it's important to note that not only can you choose to take your parents with you another time, but you can also invite everyone along to celebrate the entire family unit. You may also want to start doing vacations on a more spread-out basis (so you can go abroad again with other family members) and try to include everyone on an alternating basis. However, if someone makes you feel guilty for inviting your in-laws on a family vacation when you want to strengthen and maintain that relationship, communication is in order. You need to communicate your boundaries and your need for a relationship with them. Do not allow toxic opinions to dictate your relationships.

Secondly, difficulties can arise merely from the extravagance of these vacations and the fact that it's with family. Let's face it, traveling with family in general as an adult can be stressful. However, understand that introducing your in-laws to experiences they may not experience otherwise can be an incredibly rewarding and enriching experience. It's a chance to create cherished memories across the globe and discover completely unchartered territory together. This not only strengthens your familial bond but helps you all grow individually in your personal journey. Traveling abroad may take careful planning, but it is an opportunity to open the door to other cultures or ideals that you may not experience on the regular. When you plan a trip internationally, it is important to ensure that everyone has a fulfilling and enjoyable experience. It is important that we take essential steps and strategies for a fun time for everyone. This is everything from choosing the right destination to striking the perfect balance between new experiences and comfortable ones. Here are a few tips to get you started.

- **Choose locations carefully.** Getting your in-laws on board is often as simple as finding out where they want to go. However, it's not always as easy as asking them, especially if they're the type to go with the flow or who is eager to please everyone. If they are like that, it may be up to you to come up with something. In order to do that, think about what they might enjoy. Maybe they're history buffs with a special interest in World War II. Maybe they love going to the theater together. Or maybe their ancestors came from another country, a country they may want to visit. Have they ever mentioned something like an African safari or seeing Egyptian pyramids? Try to find some interests and go from there.

- **Pick an easier location if it's the first big trip for them or they're not used to traveling.** Baby steps are usually a good idea with novice travelers of any age. A DIY trip through India, for instance, might be a more challenging adventure for many travelers. It may be better to start small. Instead, opt for a place without a language barrier. For those who aren't quite as adventurous, potentially look at places with familiar foods. The fewer things pushing your in-laws out of their comfort zone, the more likely they may be to try something new along the way. Cruises can be a good option because they cater to a multitude of different people at any given time. Also, your in-laws can enjoy excursions and adventure during the day and then come back to the familiarity of the ship afterward. This option can also help when dealing with finances because a majority of the expenses are paid beforehand.

- **Start slow.** As stated, baby steps. Although you may not think it's worth the long flight for a trip that's shorter than two weeks, if your in-laws are embarking on their first international trip, you should probably start with something shorter. A five-to-seven-day trip in one place with a day trip or two may be a better option unless you have particularly adventurous in-laws. Think of it like the sampler platter at a new restaurant you go to: they'll get to try a few things so that they know better what suits them for the next time. This is great because it prevents them from being completely overwhelmed by too much all at once.

- **Figure out the budget and finances ahead of time.** Are you fronting the entire bill for this? It's essential to be clear about finances before you head out. As awkward as discussions about money can be with your family, they're still necessary to have before a big trip. If you want to treat them to an international trip, that's wonderful—but if you're not paying for everything, it's critical to make sure they know that and to ensure that they can afford the trip. Decide before you book anything who is paying for what!

- **Don't over-schedule your days.** Even if you don't think you're a fast-paced traveler, chances are good that you'd pack more into a day than your in-laws might have done on their own. Travel can be overwhelming and incredibly exhausting even when it's great.

    ◦ Remember that everyone benefits from being well-rested. No one wants to vacation with someone who's grouchy because they're tired or hungry!

    ◦ If you're touring a museum or doing something strenuous in the morning, leave the afternoon open. If you've got plans to have a late dinner and see a show, allow for sleeping in or naps (or both) earlier in the day. Make sure everyone is well-fed and well-rested.

○ It's also important to note any mobility issues your in-laws may have. Even if they're still spry, spending a whole day walking on cobblestone streets can be hard on joints. Consider their regular schedule at home and how much more active you'll all be when traveling, and plan accordingly.

- **Get everyone involved in the planning stage.** This is the one time that you can't just let someone say, "Whatever you want to do is fine!" Make sure everyone going on your trip has input and talks about what they want to do. Top priorities need to be included in the itinerary. Make it happen. No matter what you have to do to get the feedback, do it. Even if you have to initiate every planning session. Even if you have to send them links to articles or drop off guidebooks to them. Make sure they look, research, and let you know anything they'd like to do. This alleviates surprises during the trip and also makes everyone feel represented!

- **Plan as much as possible in advance.** Whether or not you're the type of traveler who plans ahead, it's an important thing to keep in mind when taking your in-laws on any trip, especially one abroad. It will mean less wasted time during the trip going back and forth on the topic of what to do every day. It means you can book skip-the-line tours so no one has to stand for hours outside any given attraction. It means everyone knows (and approves of) the itinerary in advance and isn't surprised at the last minute with something they don't want to do.

- **Balance new experiences with comfortable ones.** For many of us, learning and experiencing new things is one of the biggest perks of traveling. That doesn't have to change when you bring your family along for the ride, even if they're a bit less adventurous than you are. You likely have a good sense of where your in-laws' comfort zones are and what might be pushing it too far. Find ways to make sure they're not spending too much time being uncomfortable. This can be achieved by proper balance. Go out to eat that adventurous meal for lunch and opt for a more familiar dinner. And on the flip side, if they're more adventurous than you are, be open to trying things but make sure they opt for something a little milder afterward. You never know; they may push you into doing something you might not have done otherwise. Balance makes sure that all of you are happy!

- **Plan some alone time.** This may sound counter-intuitive to going on a vacation with your in-laws, but it is a good idea to carve out a little alone time—or, more specifically, alone time with your partner. See if they wouldn't mind doing one activity while you and your spouse do another. Or maybe you guys want to hang back while they go to that museum down the street. Either way, just plan one or two things during the trip that you can do on your own (or with your partner). This is particularly important if you live a bit further away from your in-laws and haven't spent a lot of time with them in recent years. During a week-long trip, you may want to plan a day in the middle where you all get a break from one another. After all, everyone needs a chance to reset their clock. This is especially true if there are introverted family members in the mix.

- **Keep everyone in mind.** This may be the most important— and most difficult—thing to keep in mind. You worked hard for those vacation days and saved up to go on this trip, and the last thing you want is to come home disappointed. When you decide to introduce international travel (or even domestic travel) to your in-laws, you're signing on to take them on a trip that suits them as well. Depending on your in-laws, that might mean hotels instead of hostels, taxis instead of walking, museums instead of nightclubs, and more sit-down restaurants than street food. The perfect trip is out there for both you and them. And you never know, they may just surprise you with how much adventure they're willing to have!

Get Photos Made With Them

We discussed a little of this earlier in the guide. However, this truly is a great way to celebrate the good times! Your family portraits bring your family together. It reminds your family of its love for one another. Your family portraits bring joy. In hard times, your family portraits can bring comfort and can heal. Think about when your in-laws pass. Having photographs of them can truly help you, your partner, and the children heal from the experience by reminiscing on positive times.

Another reason why family portraits are so important is that merely having them hung up in your home can increase your children's self-esteem. Studies show that having your family photographed and having loving portraits displayed somewhere proudly in your home sends the message that your family is important to one another. It shows your children that they are important to you. By including their grandparents/your in-laws, you show them that their entire family matters.

These photographs are an eternal reminder of your family as it is in a single moment. It honors the memories you've created together and also gives you something beautiful to look at. Photographers are especially good at capturing images that you wouldn't likely be able to capture otherwise, and they pose you and your family members in a way that accentuates your figures. Having portraits taken provides fun experiences that you will all remember that also live on in candid-style photographs for years to come.

The philosophy is simple: it's important to show a family as a pure unit. The photographer's job is to create an atmosphere so that this unit can thrive and come across on film in a way that is incredible.

Clue Them in on Achievements and Future Goals

Life is a journey filled with accomplishments and milestones. Celebrate your in-laws' achievements the same as you would your parents', and also allow them to celebrate with you when you reach your own and your children's.

Make sure you not only celebrate the milestones themselves but also celebrate how they help you achieve your goals when you do. That recognition sometimes means the world! For example, thank them for being a support to you when you graduate college, or for watching the kids all those late nights you had to put in at work to get your promotion. Whatever you feel they've done for you, make sure you recognize that and celebrate the good times as often as possible.

Don't forget that it's not just you who is capable of reaching milestones! They may be older, but they could have their own set of accomplishments worth celebrating. Celebrate that promotion they just got; celebrate their retirement; celebrate that big purchase they just made. Whatever achievement they have reached, recognize it, and celebrate it. Likewise, continue to grow your relationship by letting them know when you meet your successes and goals so they can celebrate with you! It is important to let them know when you're doing well so they aren't only there for you in the tough times, but also for the good. Let them flood you with love. Doing these things together is a powerful way to celebrate life in general—but also celebrate everyone's achievements and the good times you have together as a family *and* individually.

Share Life-Altering Moments with Them (Even the Bad Ones)

It's easy to share good news. That new promotion, that big car or home purchase, the baby you and your partner are expecting—these are all exciting and easy to share. But make sure you're being real with your in-laws and parents. Tell them when you lose your job, when you're having trouble paying bills and you think something financially detrimental may happen, or when you feel like you're a failure as parents.

Although it may be embarrassing or you may feel too much pride to share, keep in mind that it's the best thing to do for your relationships. Sharing your life moments with your family brings you closer together. Not only can they offer their advice to you, but they can also be a shoulder to lean on in times of distress. Being vulnerable with others truly allows for bonds to develop and become richer. It allows for moments of celebration to become heightened when good times come back around.

Key Takeaways

In Chapter 7, we emphasize the importance of including in-laws in family celebrations and traditions. The chapter suggests commemorating special occasions like Father's Day and Mother's Day as opportunities to show appreciation and build connections with your partner's parents while maintaining that you don't have to forget your own parents or your own plans (if you're a parent).

Additionally, the chapter highlights the significance of maintaining old traditions while introducing new ones that resonate with all family members. It offers practical tips for hosting in-laws, such as inviting them over for dinner and letting them contribute to the meal.

The chapter also discusses the complexities of traveling with in-laws, emphasizing the need for careful planning. Remember to choose locations carefully, pick an easier trip to begin with, figure out budget and finances ahead of time, don't over-schedule your days, get everyone involved in the planning stage., balance new experiences with comfortable ones, plan some alone time, and keep everyone in mind.

The chapter also discusses the significance of having professional photographs made with your loved ones. Not only is the experience one to celebrate, but the photographs will allow you all an opportunity to celebrate your lives together and the bond you possess for years to come.

And finally, share your present and future achievements with one another, including the negative moments. Being vulnerable with them truly allows the bond you have with your in-laws to develop and become even richer.

Chapter 8
Final Thoughts

As we come to the final chapter in this journey to provide *50 Ways to Love Your In-Laws*, it's essential to reflect on the path we've traveled to explore the intricate dance of love and what it can mean no matter the dynamic.

Throughout this book, we have delved into the significance of understanding how to communicate effectively, grow bonds with our in-laws, and cultivate that bond for years to come. Love truly is a dynamic and evolving force that connects us in ways we can never truly predict. Your in-laws are human beings, and those human beings are complex and beautiful.

Fostering a successful relationship is not about finding the perfect formula or mastering a set of guidelines. Instead, it's about the dedication and effort we put into nurturing the unique bonds we have with our loved ones. Your in-laws will appreciate the steps you have taken to communicate with and understand them in a way that creates a lasting relationship. They will appreciate you making them a priority.

The Importance of Continuous Effort and Growth in Relationships

Our journey together in this book has underscored the importance of continuous effort and growth in relationships. Love is not a static concept but a force that thrives on the energy we invest in it. Every day, we have the opportunity to learn, adapt, and grow in our relationships. Our personalities evolve, and our needs change. To be our happiest selves we must communicate with one another, focus on ourselves and our significant others, and continue to maintain self-growth as well as growth within our relationships.

Embracing the Nature of Love and Understanding

Love is not a one-size-fits-all concept. It is as diverse and complex as the human beings who experience it. Through the pages of this book, we've learned that there is no right or wrong way to love. It is important to celebrate one another's differences and embrace the individuality of each person and every relationship by offering positivity, understanding, and respect.

Learning Through Differences

The differences between people and relationships create an opportunity to truly develop patience, understanding, and empathy, especially when we focus on each other's individual emotional strengths. In learning to love your in-laws, you have expanded your horizons, broadened your perspective, and hopefully even given yourself more tools and resources needed to deepen your relationship with your in-laws. Embrace the commonalities you share as well as the differences you possess in emotional strengths. Learn from them and enhance your own emotional strengths. These are critical in balancing relationship dynamics.

Cherish Your Love

As we conclude this book, it is important to leave you with the encouragement to continually evolve, adapt, and cherish the love you have for your family as a whole, including your in-laws. Use the knowledge and insights gained from this guide as tools for strengthening the bond you have with them.

It is quite easy to begin to take someone for granted, especially after growing comfortable with them or you find yourself moving in an opposing direction for one reason or another. Over time, it is natural to stop saying "thank you" as often or to stop appreciating things they do for you. This leads to eventually devaluing one another. This leads to no longer cherishing one another.

Never stop cherishing your loved ones. You have a finite amount of time with them. If you can, pretend every day is a new day to find a way to show your appreciation and imprint on their lives. Use the guidelines of this book to understand their needs and desires and how to continue to make them smile as often as possible

Stay Curious

Curiosity doesn't kill the cat; it keeps the cat interesting, and it keeps the world around it interesting. Stay curious about yourself and stay curious about the people you love, and you will never become bored or stop trying to make time for them.

Start with yourself. Never stop learning about and working on yourself. It's easy to focus on others' shortcomings and overlook your personal struggles. Hopefully, as you learn more about your own motivations, areas of strength and struggle, and unmet desires or needs that you may have, you develop a new curiosity to discover more truth as well as improve on any shortcomings you may have.

When you place your in-laws on equal footing to yourself and realize that they're people too, you begin to realize it is quite natural to have shortcomings. However, it is a joy to realize that they also have strengths in areas that you may not have realized before, and you can now look forward to finding out more about them.

See yourself. See your family.

Explore one another. Meet in a moment of mutual discovery to grow closer and create a stronger bond with one another. Since none of you should ever stop growing, there should always be something new to discover about one another during your many family moments.

Make Time

Of course, being curious and discovering more about one another will take quite a bit of time and investment. So, take the time! There will be inconsistency as you all continue your journey through this life. This happens for a lot of different reasons, but mostly it happens as you transition into new seasons of life. These are times of so much chaos and so much change that it is easy to feel spread thin as it is. Prioritize your relationship with your family. This is why your regular check-ins are so important. Ask one another, "Are we making enough time for each other?" It may seem obvious, but that small gesture will open you all up to being honest about whether you feel properly invested in.

There are times that you need time to talk about the nitty-gritty or the "business" of your family, but there will also be times that one of you just needs time to vent or emotional support. In those moments, all of you need to understand something: togetherness is what matters. Remember, you are going through this life with each other. Make the time with them to ensure that it's a fun, compassionate, healthy, and emotionally fulfilling life. Moments of laughter and silliness or shared activity can bring such a bond of closeness at the end of the day. So always make the time. No matter their love language or their personality, others, like you, crave precious quality time together. Love, at its core, is all about being present in the moments you share. Make the time, cherish each other, and embrace the ever-evolving journey of love.

Remember to live in the moment, enjoy your family, and respect the values that your family unit is founded upon. Work at being the healthiest (mentally and physically) you can be in order to truly love—including, and quite especially, your in-laws!

About the Author

Dr. Sarah Cline lives with her husband, two daughters, two German Shepherds, and two Yorkies in the hills of North Carolina. Her expertise in relationship-building has offered her the opportunity to travel around the world as a keynote speaker and international workshop facilitator.